UNDERSTANDING
SONSHIP

"The Master Key to Unlock Your Destiny"

Hubert S. Hategekimana

King's Way Media
40 Henderson Ave
Ottawa - ON K1N 7P1
CANADA

ISBN: 978-0-9959245-0-5

Printed in the United States of America
First Edition Printing: April 2017

DEDICATION

First and foremost, I would like to dedicate this book to Our Father, the giver and sustainer of my life. I am nothing without you and you are the only Lord of my life.

To My Chilla [Jenny], I could not have been able to do this work if you were not as supportive as you are—you make my life so easy, I do not even know how to describe the gift you are to me. I understand more and more why he who finds a wife has found a good thing, a blessing from the Lord. Thank you for just being you, Jenny, I love you!

To my children, the reason I wrote this book, the blessings of our lives—thanks for allowing me to better understand what being a father is. You are my treasure, Kayla, Ketsia and Klemes, I love you my babies.

Sandra, my big sister, thanks for taking care of everyone around you! Your generosity is amazing. Because of your availability, I can travel the world in peace because I know you have my back. Thanks for all you do for us; we do not take it for granted.

To my Dad, Evariste, and Mom, Veronique, you are the parents anyone could dream of. Through the hard and easy times, you always looked out for our benefit. Thank you for the example of hard work and righteousness in all endeavors. You supported me as much as you could, even if most of the time you did not understand nor agree with what I was doing. You gave birth to me and I will always honor both of you.

To grand papa Jean and grand mama Clotilde, you are the best in-laws anyone could hope for. Thanks for your love and support.

To my big brother, Alexis, and younger sisters Sabine and Fortunee, thanks for your love and support. I know I can always count on all of you.

Titie and Regine, my beloved sisters, I am so proud of the young ladies you are becoming. It does not matter where you start, but where you finish. From Nyakaziziri to what you are accomplishing now is just amazing. I will see you at the top!

Kolbe, my younger brother, I am so proud of the man you are becoming. Your gift will make room for you.

To Pauline and the Simonet, thank you for changing my life. You brought me from Rwanda and gave me the opportunity to become international. You allowed me to experience what was not even in my wildest dream

To my extended family, thank you for your love, support and encouragement.

Papa Graham and Mama Leslie, thanks for adopting me and my family. Thank you for your true love and support! Your adoption started this journey and I will forever be grateful for introducing me to Dr. Munroe.

Dr. Myles Munroe, my beloved mentor (A.K.A Papa), you adopted and treated me like one of your own without being able to even pronounce my last name correctly. You would give a new version of my name every time you called me in public and I think you did that on purpose (I hope you are smiling from heaven). I miss hearing you say every time you would see me, "Where is your wife?" and "My beloved son." I think I finally get what you meant when you told me that I was a genius but did not know it. I got it Papa, and now I know it! I will make your voice louder than it was when you were alive, and yes Papa, I am not a dumb African! How I miss all of the jokes around dinner and conversations after events – all of the wisdom and insight.

Now it is up to us to make sure that what you taught us in private can be seen in public by our work. You said that the quality of a leader is seen by what happens after he is gone. I will make sure that my life will prove that you were the greatest leader of our generation!

Mama Ruth, you lived to strengthen marriages and families. Thank you for investing in my wife and her friends. I will make sure that our family makes you proud.

Diego, my irreplaceable brother, I miss your hard work and dedication to the advancement of the Kingdom of God. You were a great seer and a forerunner. You saw this book in me before I could see it myself. I remember the late nights on trips and I miss our long phone calls planning on how to take the Kingdom message into the Third World nations across Africa and Latin America. I miss your crazy ideas; but what I miss the most is your true love and support! You believed in me before I could believe in myself. Because you were a true seer, you saw things most of us could not grasp. Thanks for being my prophet. I am glad I was privileged enough to spend the last weeks of your life on earth with you on the land of my ancestors, my beloved East Africa, doing what we were born to do and you got a chance to spend time with my family. We all love and miss you dearly!

Doc and Frakhan, thank you for taking care of me on the road and when I was in Nassau. Thank you for the stories and encouragements. Doc, I hold tight to the words you told me in Houston when we spent the whole night talking in the lobby. Your stories were truly impactful – rest well.

Finally, I dedicate this book to all of my fathers, teachers, friends, spiritual sons and mentees. It is because of all of your contributions to my life that writing this book was possible.

UNDERSTANDING SONSHIP

TABLE OF CONTENTS

ENDORSEMENTS

This work by Hubert Sugira is an excellent resource and tool on the subject of sonship. It is obvious that he has done extensive research and combined it with his personal experience to ensure that the reader leaves with an expansive comprehension of the subject. Not only does he explain "sonship," but he outlines the levels of relationships that produce "sonship" and the fact that "sonship" is not simply a gender based issue but a spiritual principle outlined in the Bible and emphasized by Jesus. He also, like many of us who were impacted by the late Dr. Myles Munroe, uses the fatherly knowledge and advice gleaned from Dr. Munroe to further explain the principle and make it personal. This resource is highly recommended for every Kingdom Citizen and truth seeker.

Dr. Dave Burrows
Senior Pastor and President, Bahamas Faith Ministries Fellowship
and Bahamas Faith Ministries International
(Founded by the late Dr. Myles Munroe)

There are so many books out there about so many topics and by so many authors, but not enough books about an important subject like this. In *Understanding Sonship*, Hubert brings to light in such a compelling way, the divine concept behind the creation of the universe, the existence of mankind and the Kingdom of God. The passion, with which it is written, coupled with the depth of wisdom it offers, truly makes it a master key that will unlock your destiny.

Alex Ihama
Speaker, Coach, Consultant on Leadership and Strategic Management
Author of *Mystique of Leadership*
President - International School of Greatness
Toronto, Canada

Hubert Hategekimana is a young man called from the bowels of genocide in Rwanda where thousands of families were torn apart to be a voice for our Father on the subject of sonship. Hubert methodically reveals through this book the journey necessary to be a faithful son through his own life with his father. It is more than theory to this young man, it is a reality of his life and how it molded him into the man and father he is today.

I commend him for his honesty on this subject as well as the many hours he placed inside this book to bring revelation to all of us in a time when many are fatherless.

Thank you Hubert; you were born for such a time as this. What you have walked through in your life has been used as a great tempering tool. You are a sharp instrument that God will used to thresh the nations in the coming years.

Dr. Karen Spano
Senior Pastor of Zion Life Diplomat Center
Founder and President - WEEPs International
Presidential Stateswoman with I Change Nations
Trustee - International Third World Leadership Association

In this book, Hubert approaches a theme that is sometimes forgotten. While we were in Freeport Grand Bahamas, I heard him say a phrase that caught my attention until today, "The sons need to amend the errors of their fathers." Hubert has demonstrated a deep intellectual understanding of the role of Sonship. Through his life, he had two good role models, his biological father Evariste Hategekimana and the late Dr. Myles Munroe, his spiritual father. Through these two individuals, he learned how to be a devoted son and serve them with his gift. I have the total confidence, that this book will be a great tool full of keys and principles, to help us understand the gift of being sons, adopted by God.

Carlos Seise
Tenor

Hubert's book cites the role of Andrew as the connector of Jesus and several of his followers. It was our privilege to meet Hubert when he was one of the hundreds of mentees of Dr. Myles Munroe's online program and to personally introduce him and his story to Dr. Munroe. As Hubert progressed in his sonship journey, we have been first hand witnesses to:

- the trust Hubert gained with Dr. Munroe through testing,

- the price Hubert was willing to pay to be mentored,

- Hubert's stepping up as a son to serve his father's vision by web streaming Dr. Munroe's messages to millions around the world, and

- his building for his father's legacy, having been adopted, trained, corrected, covered, and given an inheritance from his father.

You will drink deeply from the truths in this book, soaking in Godly wisdom and understanding to facilitate your discovery and development of your own purpose and legacy through the experience of sonship.

Graham and Leslie Pitt
30 year Trustees - International Third World Leaders Association

"The author clearly articulates a unique understanding of Sonship as a concept. In essence, the big picture of leadership starts with purpose, executes in sonship and completes in legacy for the next generation. This is living your life to the fullest. A great read by Hubert Sugira Hategekimana. I commend this work to the world."

Dr The Honorable Kendal Major, MP
Speaker of the House of Assembly/Conference Chairman
Nassau, N.P., The Bahamas

Understanding Sonship is masterfully written delving into purpose, sonship and legacy. Nothing in life is successfully accomplished without purpose. No one successfully succeeds in life without a mentor, and lastly our lives are not complete until we have left a legacy to the next generation. I commend Hubert Sugira Hategekimana on the outstanding work in this book.

Dr. Sylvia Jordan
Politician, Author, Entrepreneur

In a culture steeped in short cuts and rebellion against authority, Hubert brilliantly lays out this fundamental, yet invaluable time-tested principle. Sonship is one of the most misunderstood and undervalued truths that must be activated in order to achieve maximum and sustainable success in one's life assignment. Each chapter carefully walks you through the process of sonship as it is the chief ingredient in unlocking one's dormant destiny. I can personally testify to the measured results in my life by simply applying this master key. I am personally grateful to Hubert for writing this soon to-be-classic book for the hundreds of thousands that will benefit from it. The wise will learn and apply.

Trista Sue Kragh
Hotelier, Author, International Speaker
Founder – Kingdom Community International
President – Agents For Change

This book taps into the heart and mind of God concerning the Father-Son relationship in the Kingdom of God. I know of some books written from a father to son's perspective, but none from the heart of a submissive son who has experienced the blessings and benefits of such a relationship.

Dr. Darrell Wilson
Apostle/Senior Pastor
Acts Church Ministries International

This book on sonship is both revelatory and relevant. In these pages you'll find the truth on how the Kingdom of God advances people straight from the Father's Word. Spiritual father son relationships are imperative to the development of your purpose through the connection and the priority of Sonship.

Hubert knows from experience the meaning of sonship and has shared this truth hidden in these pages. When read and applied, it will certainly catapult your life.

Dr. Jermone Glenn
The Revolution Culture Movement

The world has seen many changes. The fast expansion of technologies; the massive growth of economies; the amazing interconnections; and much-improved well being. Yet, the world is witnessing horrible setbacks, from stubborn poverty patterns, wars and conflict, racism and sexism. While many ideas have been tried with limited success. It is now time for solutions that fixes the human problem, the problem of misalignment of human endeavors and their God-given purposes. In this book, Hubert shares time-tested insights into pursuit of purpose through the principle of sonship. Thus, the book reveals a kingdom framework for fundamental change that the world has been waiting for.

Siphamandla Zondi, DPhil.
Professor of International Relations
University of Pretoria
South Africa

ACKNOWLEDGEMENTS

I would like to express my gratitude to the many people who saw me through this book; to all those who provided support, talked things over, read, wrote, offered comments, endorsed my work, allowed me to quote their remarks, and assisted in editing, proofreading, and design.

Above all, I want to thank my wife, Jenny and the rest of my family, who supported and encouraged me in spite of all the time it took me away from them. I know it was a long and difficult journey for you.

I would like to thank "mum," Leslie, and Papa, Graham. Your adoption started the journey that led to this book; thank you for your love and support.

Carlos and Char Seise, thank you for making it possible for me to travel with Dr. Munroe and to be able to serve.

Trista Sue Kragh, thank you for pushing me to write this book.

Stacey Flowers, thank you for literally bringing this work out of me.

Debra Horner, thank you for making sure that everything was in order. You rock! What would we do without you?

Karen Spano, thank you for your wisdom and input on sonship.

Phyllis Redman, thank you for your work and dedication for this book to come to completion; you are the embodiment of sonship.

April Dobson, thank you for the counsel, edits, and support; this work could not have been finalized for publication without you.

David Süveges, thank you for coming in during the last stages and giving it your all. I am in awe of your level of dedication and understanding. You will go far in life.

Achie McEachern, thank you for all the late edits, input, and adding your final touches.

Josias Kue, thank you for all your support and help with graphics over the years

Joseph Semaan, thanks for your mentorship, friendship, and for believing in me. My life has been impacted by your desire to see everyone around you succeed and to change people's lives.

To Grace Uwamahoro, you are the first person who paid the price for my life to change; my life is the fruit of your labor to birth me into the Kingdom of God. You taught me to love the word of God and to read the bible for myself. From the beginning, you laid a great foundation for me.

To Pastor Alexis Bubanje and the Racheté church family, you were my first Kingdom family; you thought me to love God and people. You came into my life when I was at my lowest and showed me what true love was! I'm grateful for everything you did for me and my family.

To Aimable Ntaganda, what can I say and where do I begin? You have been an angel sent into my life when I could not do anything for myself. You were a mother, father, friend, and brother all in one. Words cannot express my gratitude. I will just stick with thank you! May you reap what you sowed into my life

My Pastor and my father Arsène Poungui, thank you for being the first one to believe in my potential, thank you for your unconditional love and corrections.

To the Élus family, my church, thank you for your patience, correction, and for the opportunity to serve you and refine my gift.

Last but not least, I beg forgiveness from all of you who have been with me over the course of the years and whose names I have failed to mention. You are dear to me.

FOREWORDS

I talk to people all of the time who are struggling. Struggling to find purpose, struggling to earn money, struggling to find love, and even struggling to find themselves. People wonder aimlessly through life looking for the similitude of success, desperately searching to find solid ground. This search seems to be never ending, tired, broken people who are exhausted and broken but have no answers that solve their problems.

I am often approached by the people I have just described and am asked for my advice on how they can move forward. How can I find the solution to this issue? When I am asked these questions, I typically respond with another question. That question is; "Who do you trust, listen to with the intent to obey?"

I can already see your face as you read my words. It never fails that the look I get is a cross between bewilderment, astonishment, and the plain "are you serious" look. Most people want you to solve their problem in a quick, few minute conversation; but that is not the way it happens. To have a great life, you need great relationships.

So, why would I ask a troubled person such a question? Well, it is because trusting someone enough to do what they say is the key to success. This is exactly why Hubert wrote this book. When you find someone to listen to who has the success you want and they are willing to birth you into it, your life is about to change. I have heard people say, "I have a lot of mentors." When they say this I ask, but which one do you trust to obey?

This is called fatherhood. Fatherhood is the key to your success. Fatherhood is the avenue that transfers the tools to succeed in life. Fatherhood makes sure the generations continue in progress, one great generation after another.

As a matter of fact, fatherhood is the foundation of the Kingdom of God. Fatherhood is the system that God has chosen to be the bedrock of how His Kingdom expands and keeps its attributes. I can explain this in at least three ways. First of all, He calls Himself Father. He does not say that He is mother or brother, He is Father. Second, He calls us sons. We are His offspring. We are not slaves or servants, because slaves and servants cannot inherit the father's house. Thirdly, the phrases "his son" or "his sons" are mentioned about 350 times in the scripture, dependent upon which translation you use. Here's one of the best examples in Exodus 27:21.

> *"In the tabernacle of meeting, outside the veil which is before the Testimony, Aaron and his sons shall tend it from evening until morning before the LORD. It shall be a statute forever to their generations on behalf of the children of Israel."*

Hubert has done an awesome job exposing the importance of Sonship/fatherhood. He walks us through the knowledge trail of why we need fathers and how to connect to them.

Obviously, there are people who have never known their natural father. That does not mean that there are no fathers around that cannot help you discover and complete your destiny.

I will never forget the day I laid eyes on Hubert. He was standing next to my spiritual father, Dr. Myles Munroe, on the platform at Dr. Munroe's international leadership conference. As Dr. Munroe described his life, it was almost unbelievable, that this young man had survived the genocide in Rwanda and lost many family members. But he had to hide out for weeks and months in the bush to preserve his life. But somehow, he had gotten a hold of Dr. Munroe's material and was introduced to the kingdom of God. After Dr. Munroe introduced him, the evidence of the kingdom was upon him. He said he had only been speaking English for just a few weeks and was trying very hard to articulate how much learning the kingdom had meant to him. To me, it was more than just the kingdom message that had an impact on this young man. It was the fact that Dr. Myles Munroe [the great leader that he was], had received Hubert as a spiritual son. I believe that this made the biggest difference in Hubert's life. He got to learn "Sonship" from the master teacher. After the untimely death of Dr. Myles Munroe, Hubert gave me a call and explained to me the customs of many African nations. He said that if the father dies, the children look to an older brother that has leadership, and submit to him as though he were the father. After saying those words, he asked me to be a spiritual father in the stead of Dr. Myles Munroe, and I accepted. This book is evidence of everything that he learned in close proximity to Dr. Munroe. I'm very proud of his work and his life.

Read this book, study it, and make a reference guide through your journey to discover fatherhood. It will become a turning point in your life.

Martin L. Williams, PhD
Senior Pastor, Ambassador Worship Center
Omaha, Nebraska

Understanding Sonship is the writings of a mastermind who, himself, has personally experienced true sonship in its purest form. The basis of this book is founded on Vision, Legacy, Succession and Love. True sonship is about a father's love toward his sons and a son's love for his father and his father's vision. When it comes to leadership and succession, love is so much more important than loyalty, commitment, devotion, dedication and faithfulness. This book will resonate greatly with many of you that have both biological and spiritual fathers. The abundant wealth of knowledge and wisdom available here on this topic is unprecedented and I look forward to its outstanding effect around the world.

From the introduction, the foundation laid before us is obviously well studied substantiating the information in the pages that follow. There are many books available on the market on Fatherhood, but hardly any books exist on this topic of Sonship; so it is refreshing to read from the perspective of sons, followers and future leader(s).

Hubert has learned so much from so many fathers that he has sat under and has earned the right and privilege to write on a topic such as this. He was one of many sons of my own father, Dr. Myles Munroe who himself has touched so many lives and has been the father to so many people. This is why there is no excuse why all of those "so many" cannot discover their purpose and vision, become great leaders and leave a legacy for generations to come.

As indicated in this book, God is always thinking about legacy and the reproduction of himself through his children. So it is imperative that we understand the key principles of sonship and true leadership alike; because even as leaders, we will never and should never stop being sons. I highly recommend this book as an excellent read to both leaders and their followers and to mentors and their mentees as a good resource and insight into the mind of God and why He created man just like Himself.

Ms. Charisa Munroe
Daughter of the late Dr. Myles Munroe
Vice President - Munroe Global/Myles Munroe International
President - Myles and Ruth Munroe Foundation
International Speaker, Television Host
Bahamas and USA

We are living in a time where the spirit of lawlessness has created such a fatherless culture that is plaguing our world and filling the prisons with men looking for fathers. This plague has unfortunately entered into the church and in the words of Paul, the apostle; we have thousands of teachers but no fathers. There are so many churches, governments, families, and nations that are suffering due to Fatherlessness. In this book, *Understanding Sonship*, Hubert carefully crafts a formula for proper elevation from sonship to fatherhood for the preservation of the next generation. The author clearly highlights the importance of the Father transitioning properly their inheritance to Sons. It gives an account of how sons must submit themselves to receive all the tools necessary for preserving the next generation. This book will teach sons and fathers the true value of legacy and the joy of purpose, destiny, and vision. The author makes it clear that submission to the process of preparation and testing will be a sure direction to releasing ones potential. An understanding of honor is one of the main focuses of this book and there are multiple examples of this principle. Once you have mastered this key of honor, you are well on your way to becoming everything that you were born to be. I commend this work and the convictions of the author, Hubert, for sharing his heart to a world that needs the succession of Fathers and the preservation of legacy. This is a must read for sons who aspire to be good Fathers in the future.

Pepe Ramnath, PhD
Research Scientist, UN-EO Ambassador
Senior Pastor, Miramar Kingdom Community Center
Miramar, Florida

INTRODUCTION

"Sonship" is the relationship between a "son and a father". Understanding and applying the principles of this relationship will allow you to pinpoint your purpose, life's vision, and fulfill your destiny. We will discover the importance of this relationship, since it is recorded in the last Book of the Old Testament as the last thing that God corrected before reconnecting mankind to its purpose in creation through His Son Christ Jesus.

As recorded in the Book of Genesis, God created man to "have dominion" "over the earth". Then God said, "Let us make mankind in our image, in our likeness, let them have dominion over the fish in the sea and the birds in the sky, over the livestock and all the wild animals, and over all the creatures that move along the ground" (Genesis 1:26). This word "dominion" is defined as "sovereign or supreme authority; the power of governing and controlling." This "dominion" referred to in the scripture is the very thing that mankind lost when the first man, Adam, made the decision to disobey God in "The Book of Genesis (The fall of Man, Genesis 3:1-21)". It is here that we read and discover the difference between the blessing given to Noah and his sons, after they came out of the ark, and the blessing God gave to Adam before the fall. In Genesis 1:28,

"God blessed them, and God said unto them, be fruitful, and multiply, and replenish the earth, and subdue it: and have dominion over the fish

of the sea, and over the fowl of the air, and over every living thing that moveth upon the earth."

As we read in Genesis 9:1-2,

"And God blessed Noah and his sons, and said unto them, be fruitful, and multiply, and replenish the earth. And the fear of you and the dread of you shall be upon every beast of the earth, and upon every fowl of the air, upon all that moveth upon the earth, and upon all the fishes of the sea; into your hand are they delivered."

Now that we have literally read the above scriptures and have definitively defined the word "dominion", we can see clearly that what humans lost in The Book of Genesis is exactly what Jesus came to reintroduce to us, according to His first public statement in Mathew 4:17: "From that time Jesus began to preach, and to say, Repent: for the kingdom of heaven is at hand."

The word translated as "Kingdom" here is the Greek word "Basileia" that means royal power, ruler ship, and Dominion. Jesus speaks and prophetically announces that He has already purchased and redeemed man. What this means is that He has purchased man and in doing so has rightfully positioned man back into his place of "dominion and authority" over the earth. He states that He has once again "stood" man back in his stance of "ruler-ship mandate" and that He (Jesus), has paved the road for all of mankind and put man back on the right path.

Through the scriptures, it appears to us that man was faced with what seems to us today, as if 400 years of silence from God must have taken place before God would introduce His Son Jesus to us in "The Bible". In this book, we base the statement above on two scriptures that are found in the last thing that God said in the Old Testament which is found in the book of Malachi 5:4-5 which states,

"Behold, I will send you Elijah the prophet before the coming of the great and dreadful day of the Lord: And he shall turn the heart of the fathers to the children, and the heart of the children to their fathers, lest I come and smite the earth with a curse."

It is also found in the 'Introduction of Jesus and His Birth which is recorded in the first book of the New Testament in Matthew chapter 1 verses 18-25. It is in the last Book of the Old Testament where we find that God states that He had to first correct the relationship between fathers and sons. It is in the first book of the New Testament, Matthew, where we find the record of the genealogy and lineage of Jesus announced and where the introduction of His coming/birth is proclaimed. These two acts take place prior to God's "Great Plan of Redemption" for mankind and it is here that this great plan unfolds and is laid out before us. It is also here that God would present His restoration to mankind and while doing so give man back his "dominion and power" over the earth. During the course of this book, I will help you begin to understand the different aspects of this important relationship so that you may begin the process of fulfilling your God given assignment and reach your "pre-determined destiny"!

EVERYONE ON EARTH IS BORN WITH A PURPOSE

Everything that exists in the universe has a specific "purpose". Even the things that we cannot see have a specific purpose. Nothing that exists in this world exists without a specific role or a divine purpose. Even when we do not know the reason why a thing exists, it still does not negate the fact that there is a reason why the thing was created. As we read in Proverbs 16:4, "The Lord God has made everything for its purpose, even the wicked for the day of trouble." Since God has informed us in "His Word" just how important man is to Him, then we can deduce that if everything that exists has a specific purpose, then how much more so would God have been mindful to place in each man his own unique and miraculous purpose as well. Just as God purposed everything on earth that He created, He has also done so with every man. Today there are more than seven billion people living on this grand planet that the Lord created and each one of us exists for a specific reason. No matter what the circumstances of one's birth, no one exists by pure coincidence, accident, chance or happen stance. You were created by "The Living God" with a specific purpose in mind and the good news is that no matter what your life has been thus far, there is a reason why you are still breathing today. Your purpose, the reason that you were born, is embedded in the original intention that the Creator had in His mind for your life. It is the precise reason for your creation and your existence. Your purpose is the thing that made you necessary. It is the idea that preceded your creation. I share this with you now, just in case you are not already aware of this fact that "God finishes everything before He starts a thing". According to Isaiah 46:9-10,

> "Remember the former things of old: for I am God, and there is none else; I am God, and there is none like me. Declaring the end from the beginning, and from ancient times the things that are not yet done, saying, purpose shall stand, and I will do all my pleasure."

God sets up the end before He even begins the beginning. Your "purpose" is the end product for which God began your life. Simply put your purpose is the "WILL" of God for your life.

We can also say it this way "that your purpose is your destination— or should I say your "purpose" is your "destiny". Let me state it this way: if your purpose is the reason that you exist, then discovering and fulfilling your purpose should be your number one priority. The "purpose" of anything can only be found in the mind of its creator. Which is also why for you to discover your purpose and to discover the "why of your life" you must go back to your "Creator" God for Him to impart to you the revelation and understanding of the "why" you were created. The scripture says in 1 Corinthians 2:9-10 that things God prepared for those who love Him, no one has ever seen, nor heard, or even thought about, and such things can only be revealed to us by His Spirit; because only the Spirit can search into the deep things of God. The reason Jesus died was so that we could be reconciled back to God; Jesus did not die so, that we all could one day go to heaven, as many may think; but rather, Jesus came and died so that we could all discover our "purpose" and fulfill it. Jesus came to the world so that we could discover our life's work; our assignment. We are not only meant to one day discover our "purpose" but it is also meant for us to fulfill our purpose as well.

Ephesians 2:10 states, "For we are God's handiwork, created in Christ Jesus to do good works, which God prepared in advance for us to do." According to that verse, God has already prepared for everyone some "work" to accomplish and Jesus came and died so that we could get back on the right track and discover our work, our life's assignment and accomplish it. Success in this life is not measured by how many great things that you are doing or the magnitude in which you are doing them. Every product is only successful when it has accomplished the purpose for which it was made in the first place. You are only successful when you fulfill God's purpose for your life or when you have done the work your "Creator" created you to do. Nor is success measured by how many things you have done compared to what others have done or are doing. True success in this life is measured and determined by what you have done, based on what you should have done, based on the "purpose" for which you were created. Many people think that God created us only to worship Him, to pray to Him, to try to not sin while we are waiting to go to heaven et cetera and that is it. However, these ideas are contrary to what God says we are to do in His Word. Man, is first introduced in the Book of Genesis 1:26. Here it shows that God created all of us to have "dominion and ruler ship over all of His creations on this earth". He created us to have "dominion" over everything that He created, except for one another. God also created us to have some "responsibility" over all He created.

We can clearly see in the "Word of God" that He is more interested in us finishing the work that He created us to do so much so that He goes on to say in Mathew 7:21, "Not everyone who says to me, 'Lord, Lord,' will enter the kingdom of heaven, but only the one who does the will of my Father who is in heaven." God states that referring to Jesus as "Lord" is not merely enough for us to enter the "Kingdom of God" but that only those of us who do "His will" will be able to enter

"His Kingdom". The word translated as "will" in most of the English versions of the Bible is derived from the Greek word Thelēma. Thelēma means purpose, intent, what one wishes or has determined shall be done. God desires that you and I fulfill "His will" so much so that He Himself became a human to show us "what to do and how to do it". God Himself paid the unimaginable price to enable us to do His will by accomplishing and fulfilling our "purpose" on this earth. In the only public prayer of Jesus we can see that "giving God the glory" is not determined by singing unto Him but it is rather done so by giving unto Him the completion of the work He sent us here to do. Jesus states in John 17:4, "I glorified you on earth by completing the work you gave me to do." You can only begin to glorify God when you discover "the works" He has prepared specifically for you to do. The works that caused Him to create you in the first place. The works that He expects you and me to accept and to follow the process of fulfilling His predetermined work for our lives.

The word "glory" comes from the Greek word "kabod" which is defined as "the fullness of nature." The "glory of God" has been perceived as smoke or vapor. Other times it has been described as a shout, passing out, or shaking uncontrollably and falling on the ground because of the weight of that glory but in reality it is the weight of His nature on you. "Giving God the glory" is to fully manifest all of Him within you. Each one of us has a different piece of God to show to the world and when everyone operates to the fullness of His nature in us, it is then that we begin to come together as one. It is then that He our Lord and King is fully manifested in "His glory" on this earth and in this world.

Know that your purpose, your life assignment is always longer than your lifetime. God prepared your life assignment three to four generations prior to creating you. That is the reason why He says in Numbers 14:18 that those who disobey him will be punished up to the fourth generation. The fact of the matter is when you disobey God you are not only tampering with your own purpose but you are hindering many generations to come. When God needed a nation, He created the nation of Israel through the loins of Abraham. Abraham had two sons Ishmael and Isaac. Isaac was brought forth as the son of covenant, and would inherit the promises of God from his father Abraham. Isaac had two sons as well: Esau and Jacob. Of the two sons of Isaac, only Jacob would be deemed qualified to keep the promises of God. After many years, Jacob would father twelve sons who would become the twelve tribes of Israel.

Your purpose is not one single thing that you must do in your life, but rather a combination of all the works that God has prepared and imparted into you and because your purpose preceded your creation, your purpose is built on the inside of you. God has prewired you to fulfill your assignment, but the abilities you must have in order to fulfill your assignment lay dormant in you until you use them. These built-in abilities are what man refers to as "potential". They are what God the Creator knows to be "untapped power and/or unused strength" built within our DNA.

You would find that most people will argue with God when He first reveals to them "why" they were created in the first place because at that current moment they are only aware of the abilities they have already used, but God sees what they have yet to experience in their life. Only God knows what He built into each one of us and so He sees the extent of our full potential. God alone is privy to the "more within us" and whatever He calls for us to accomplish we can be assured that He has already purposed and provided for within us. Therefore, if you were to look for your purpose inside of yourself you will inevitably miss it even though it is presently there within you. You will never begin to discover what you are fully made of and the potential that already exists within you or know what is already inside of you because it is not until God places you in an environment that will trigger what He has placed within you that those "untapped abilities" are awakened and are revealed to you in an amazing way.

By the way, you are not to search for your purpose because if you focus all your energy on searching for your purpose, you will miss it. You are to seek to know the heart of your Creator and it is while doing so that He will reveal the "why" of your life to you.

HOW TO DISCOVER YOUR PURPOSE?

Purpose will manifest itself to you in two steps in your life. You will first discover "WHAT" you are supposed to do and then you will discover "HOW" you are to do it in your own unique way. Your life assignment is linked to your passion (the desires to do something), your design (natural capacity, acquired skills-potential) and your vision (your uniqueness or the distinction in what you are doing). As we move on through the chapters of this book I will show you the processes used and/or the patterns of how some of the characters in the Bible discovered and fulfilled their own divine purposes. When you are ready to discover your purpose, the Creator will put you in an environment that will trigger the potential that lies dormant on the inside of you.

It is then that you will begin to learn that what you see on the outside is only mirroring what is currently on the inside of you already. This is also where our five senses will truly kick into play. We will happen to either see, smell, hear, taste or touch something that may be a wrong or an injustice in this world that you were born to correct and that issue will wake up the potential that is and has always been lying dormant in your genes. More often than not, you may get angry or frustrated by these situations that you encounter and that you find disturbing because what you are seeing on the outside is very different from the picture of what should be and that is coded in your DNA.

We saw this happen to Moses who was created to deliver the Hebrews who were enslaved by the Egyptians. Exodus 2:11-12 states,

> "In those days, when Moses had grown up, he went out to his people and observed their hard labor, and he saw an Egyptian man attacking a Hebrew man, one of his own people. He looked this way and that

and saw that no one was there, and then he killed the Egyptian and concealed the body in the sand."

Moses had been seeing a specific injustice occur during his entire life. As a matter of fact, he himself was among those who were mistreating the Hebrews. One day something happened to him and what Moses saw outside was the projection of the struggle he had been experiencing on the inside of himself. Moses had to decide which role he should take on. You see you cannot discover your purpose when you are double minded. You must be completely sold out to God and His Kingdom to fulfill your God given purpose. Moses had been witnessing something that caused him to become very angry. He was so angry that it took him to a place that caused him to take another man's life; and if that were not enough, he did it at the expense of his own life and wellbeing. Are you willing to surrender your life when God allows you to witness the problem that you were created to solve? Are you willing to die if necessary to fulfill the purpose for which you were created?

Your purpose may not necessarily entail you losing your life physically, but it may cause you to lose advantages that you may have in your life. You may have to end some relationships, leave your job or even your own company. Perhaps you may have to leave your family like Abraham did. Sometimes God will not allow you to see what purpose He created you for because you are not ready to make the necessary sacrifices or leave your comfort zone at that time. Remember the scripture says in Matthew 16:25, "For whosoever will save his life shall lose it: and whosoever will lose his life for my sake shall find it." Life without fulfilling your purpose is not worthy of living. The late Dr. Myles Munroe used to say "the tragedy in life is not death but life without a purpose." What happened to Moses was that he saw a problem he was born to solve. Moses saw a person he was born to free; he was born to deliver people from oppression. What Moses did is the same as what most people would do when they see the problems that they are internally equipped to solve but have not received revelation from God as to "how" to fulfill their assignment.

They will try to tap into their abilities and gifts to search for solutions to the problems they see at hand, but they are not yet fully equipped to successfully resolve them. The result of this for them will be like it was for Moses--40 years of wandering around in the desert.

Forty years is not merely a number, but it represents a whole generation. Can you afford to make God lose a whole generation while you are wandering around? It may seem to you that you are doing a lot but deep inside you know that you are wandering in circles. It appears that you are busy because you are working on something but working and being productive are two totally different things. The way to know if you are being productive is measured by the level of effectiveness of your influence that you are having with others. Influence is determined by the amount of ACTION people take after they encounter your "excellent work". When you see what you are supposed to do, it is still not time for you to go and do it your way because the blueprint of your assignment is only found in the mind of your Creator and He is not necessarily counting on your strength to fulfill your life assignment. I get a bit nervous when I hear someone say that to discover your purpose you are to look inside of yourself. That you are to look at the things you love to do or the things you do easily. All of these things are the gifts you will use to fulfill your life's assignment but these elements should not be the foundation you build on to discover your purpose. You will only live a fulfilling life when you start fulfilling your life's assignment. Focusing on your gift may provide you with money, fame or power but it will never bring you the fulfillment you desire. Fulfillment in this life comes only when you are doing what you were born to do the way you were created to do it.

The other day I was thinking about famous people like Michael Jackson who seemed to have all some people dream to have. Michael was an artist who may have sold more music than any other artist will ever sell in the music industry. Michael Jackson was called the King of Pop and at the same time he died because he was so troubled that he could not sleep peacefully or rest without the aid of medication. The drugs that enabled him to sleep and that he so desperately needed were the same drugs that, in the end, would be the cause of his death. The number one thing that causes sleeplessness is a troubled mind, right? Then, how ironic is it that the very drugs that he depended on to help him sleep for a significant and amiable amount of time caused him to be addicted to them, taking control of his life and killing him. All he really wanted and needed but could not obtain with his money, riches or fame was enough "peace" that would allow his mind and body to rest. He was in dire "need" of peace that he went to the extreme measures of having a doctor inject him with enough drugs to put him into a state of relaxation that would force his body to shut down and allow his troubled mind to permit him to sleep peacefully.

How can we explain why Whitney Houston, a woman so beautiful and talented, who had obtained both fame and riches, would die by overdosing on drugs also? Why did she crave those substances? All of those things show evidence that fame or even success in what you do will not necessarily guarantee that you are fulfilling your life's assignment. Some people can be using their gifts and talents, but if they are not surrounded by the right people that care about them and their purpose, if they are not positioned in the right place and/or the proper environment where they were created to be and to thrive, then what was given to them to sustain or to be a blessing in their life, unfortunately can and may be the very thing that will lead them to their death and kill them.

I often think of how when a tree is planted in the ground it will use the sunlight for photosynthesis that will give life to the tree. However, the minute you remove it from the ground, from its source and right environment, it will begin to die. Once out of the ground and disconnected from its source, the tree will be killed by the same sunlight that was a blessing to the tree when it was in the ground and connected to its source. The same sun that was helping to sustain the plant will eventually burn the plant, and in time, will kill it. When you limit yourself to the discovery of your purpose by just assessing what your gifts are, the result will be similar to what Moses experienced, and you will end up producing death in the situation, instead of giving life. What Moses should have done was bring his anger and frustration to His Creator for answers. He should have taken it to the One who gave him life so that the Holy Spirit could show Him "how" to fix the problems he was witnessing.

This brings us to the second step. You should always go back to your Creator for guidance. Go back to the one who created you and the only one who truly knows who you are. You should always go back to God for instructions on how to correct the problem(s) that He has brought to your attention. When you reconnect to your source and seek guidance from the Holy Spirit? He will always show you "how" He initially intended for you to fix the problem.

Let us look at what Habakkuk was doing in Habakkuk 1:2-4. How did he seek guidance?

> *"How long, Lord, must I cry for help? But you do not listen! I call out to you, "Violence!" But you do not intervene! Why do you force me to witness injustice? Why do you put up with wrongdoing? Destruction and violence confront me; conflict is present and one must endure strife. For this reason, the law lacks power, and justice is never carried out. Indeed, the wicked intimidate the innocent. For this reason, justice is perverted."*

Habakkuk could barely stand to witness what was going on in his day. His heart was deeply grieved and heavy by what he was seeing. His compassion for his fellow brothers and sisters overwhelmed him. He knew in his heart that he must do something to stop the injustice he was witnessing, and he instinctively knew somehow that he must have been born to correct the issue! Habakkuk's compassion drove him to pray and to cry out to God for help. Most people only talk about how God showed Habakkuk a vision or a picture of how to correct the problem and instructed him to write it down on stones in Habakkuk 2:2, but they seem to overlook what happened in the book of Habakkuk in chapter one. Before God allows you to get a glimpse and you receive a vision of what you must do, you must first encounter the problem that your life was purposed for and that you have the solution to resolve it. You are then to bring the problem to God so that He can reveal to you "how" to resolve the problem that you now know that you have been created to solve. We see Jesus following this pattern in Matthew 9:35-38,

> *"Then Jesus went throughout all the towns and villages, teaching in their synagogues, preaching the good news of the kingdom, and healing every kind of disease and sickness. When he saw the crowds, he had compassion on them because they were bewildered and helpless, like sheep without a shepherd. Then he said to his disciples, 'The harvest is plentiful, but the workers are few. Therefore, ask the Lord of the harvest to send out workers into his harvest'."*

In this passage, Jesus encountered a problem of a lack of shepherds and He even took the time to let us know that He knows of a solution. He did not ask the disciples to go out to shepherd the crowd, but instead asked them to first seek counsel and guidance from the Lord, and ask of Him "how" the problem should be resolved. We will see how He followed this process because in the following verse of Matthew 10:1, Jesus called his twelve disciples and gave them authority over unclean spirits so they could cast them out and heal every kind of disease and sickness. The point is that He made sure to seek guidance before the implementation of the solution. This is the principle of "information and action". You do not make decisions based on information received by your senses but on the revelation you receive through your spirit.

Moses saw what he was supposed to correct. He was aware of the problems he was witnessing, but because he was only counting on his natural strength or what he already knew to do, he went ahead and used the power that he knew he had—the power that he was familiar with. Remember, Moses was a trained military chief, but the "how" God had in mind was different from the "how" Moses thought that he should respond with. We can come to this conclusion because 40 years later we read in Exodus 3:10 that when God met Moses and told him "how" He wanted Moses to deliver the people from Egypt, it was not by fighting or killing anyone, but that it was rather to simply go and talk to Pharaoh and ask him to let God's people go. Moses probably made his decision based on his upbringing, background, knowledge, prior experience, and his culture, just as most people would do today.

Like Moses, many of us will initially approach our life's assignment based on what we are naturally good at doing, our area of expertise, what we are skilled at doing, and so on. Proceeding that way is not necessarily a bad thing, but discovering how we should fulfill our God given assignment entails so much more. This is one of the many reasons why the Word of God teaches us to not lean on our own understanding but to seek Him regarding all things.

Discovering your purpose goes so far beyond one's current level of understanding, and if you seek your "how" to fulfill your purpose based on that criteria alone, you will risk limiting yourself to the capabilities and possibilities that you are aware of having. In fact, God created you to accomplish so much more than you know. The way in which one should determine their "how" should be by seeking guidance from the "Holy Spirit" to reveal exactly who you are in Him and the unlimited potential and possibilities that He built inside of you.

Initially, Moses was displeased and had a big issue with the way God instructed him to proceed, when it came to his life's assignment. Moses argued with God, saying that he was not the right person for the assignment placed before him. He thought that the "way" and the "how" by which God was instructing him to proceed would cause him to have to act out of his comfort zone, and that it would directly involve exposing Moses' weaknesses, as he had trouble speaking.

Again, I would like to stress that if you are focusing on your own understanding and your current knowledge of what you deem yourself to be good at to complete your assignment, then there is a great chance that you may miss the mark, just like Gideon almost did. You could fall short or miss the mark completely. When God appeared to Gideon and asked him to deliver his nation from the Medianites in Judges 6:14, God called for the might He had placed within Gideon, but Gideon was not aware that this ability was already placed within him when he was created. Thus, Gideon could not believe God was talking to him in such a way.

Perhaps we should move on and read about Mary's initial encounter with her purpose to get a better idea of what I am talking about here. Luke 1:26-35 states,

> *"Now in the sixth month the angel Gabriel was sent from God to a town in Galilee, named Nazareth, to a virgin who was to be married to a man named Joseph, of the family of David; and the name of the virgin was Mary. And the angel came in to her and said, Peace be with you, to whom special grace has been given; the Lord is with you. But she was greatly troubled at his words, and said to herself, what may be the purpose of these words? And the angel said to her, Have no fear, Mary, for you have God's approval. And see, you will give birth to a son, and his name will be Jesus. He will be great, and will be named the Son of the Most High: and the Lord God will give him the kingdom of David, his father: He will have rule over the house of Jacob forever, and of his kingdom there will be no end. And Mary said to the angel, how may this be, because I have had no knowledge of a man? And the angel in answer said to her, The Holy Spirit will come on you, and the power of the Most High will come to rest on you, and so that which will come to birth will be named holy, Son of God."*

Mary's assignment was to bring forth a "Son". The problem Mary initially faced was that she was not married. She was not yet married, which was the usual pattern in her day that a woman would follow prior to bringing a child into the world. It was the normal process during those times and the most sensible and easy way to have a baby.

Let us pause for a moment and play a guessing game. Can you imagine what would she have done if she was like most of us when we receive our "what", like when we receive our assignment; which in Mary's case was to conceive a child? Let us thank God that she did not act as most of us probably would have. The angel gave Mary some specific information, instruction and specification as to the gender of the child. Being a male, the bloodline and the family in which He would come from was the lineage of King David. Mary accepted her assignment and was going to start working on obeying God's instructions. Yet, while looking at her current situation, she was reminded that she was about to get married to a man from the exact same family as King David. She could have acted on her own knowledge and skillset, and have concluded in her mind that the easiest way to accomplish the task set before her by the angel would be to marry Joseph and get pregnant. By following her own understanding and heart, Mary could have acted outside of the will of God, and could have thwarted the whole plan God had designed before the beginning of time. She would have brought death to mankind instead of bringing "Life" and hope to all.

I am so happy that Mary instinctively knew to ask the right questions and remained in the "will of God" for all of mankind's sake. In Luke chapter one, we read that the Angel only told Mary "how" the plan was going to be laid out and followed through after she asked the angel for more details. When we go back and take another look at both Moses' and Mary's situations again, we notice a significant difference in how the two of them responded so differently to their life's assignments—the "what" they were both to do with their lives. Moses received the "what" of his life mission at the age of 40 and tried to fulfill what he knew to do before receiving the "how" 40 years later at the age of 80. Mary on the other hand, received both her "what and how" before doing anything on her own by asking God the right questions at the right time. Mary recognized that her assignment was much bigger than anything she could handle on her own and she immediately asked the angel "how" her assignment would be accomplished after the "what" was brought to her attention.

The scripture tells us that Moses was serving his "father" when God revealed Himself to him. Moses was pastoring Jethro's flock, his father-in-law. You will not receive your "how" until you have served someone else's vision first. Luke 16:12 states, "And if you have not been faithful in that which is another man's, who shall give you that which is your own?"

When you discover "what" the thing(s) is [are] that you were born to correct, it is not yet the time to get up and start trying to do "what" you saw you are designed to do. It is at that time that you must stop what you are doing and begin to serve someone's vision. In doing so you will be ushered into a place of what belongs to you—because it is in serving someone else's vision that you would have allowed God to show you "how" you are supposed to proceed, accomplish and fulfill your own purpose. Know that this person that you have now begun to serve is a "father" to you and to function in this "father/son" relationship you must have a clear understanding of "sonship".

To sum it up in a few words, you must discover your life's assignment or purpose. Know that God will put you into a situation where you will see or hear (encounter) a specific problem or a situation that you were intentionally created to correct. Once you get a glimpse of that understanding, you will be more than likely begin to get angry or frustrated that you may even find yourself somewhat angry at God because once you have that encounter with him – the Master of your soul, the Creator of your being, the Lord of your life – and you become aware of the situation for which you were purposefully designed for and assigned to counteract, it is then that you need to go to God and seek His divine instruction on ways to fix it! God may give you a vision. He may even reveal to you the specific "way" that He wants you to use to face the problem that He brought to your attention.

Is it at that point when you need to have most of your questions answered. Such as the with, the where, the when... We know that there is a definitive process that must be followed in order for you to discover and to fulfill your purpose. It is God's intentional, unique, divine and specifically designed purpose for your life and this process goes from "a father to his son". This book is written specifically to teach you the meaning of "Sonship" and to help you to identify and recognize your "father(s)" and provide you with the skill(s) of taking your rightful position and stance so that you are enabled to master the role of "Sonship" and are empowered with the confidence and fortitude that will not only allow but make way for you to fully unlock your destiny.

CHAPTER 1

RELATIONSHIPS

THREE RELATIONSHIP TYPES

On the journey to your destiny there are three types of people with whom you will interact. Each person you encounter in this life will to some extent fall into one of these three categories or positions: fathers, peers (friends/brothers) and sons. In this book, Fathers are defined as people that we can receive and learn from who are in specific areas, ahead of us. Fathers connect us to our past, as they are the starting point of our lives. They also pass their experiences on to us, shaping us.

Peers are people who operate at the same level; they are our friends who are also a great support for the present. Sons are those who can learn from you. They are a product of who you are and they will secure your future. It is important to recognize "who is who" because what you will receive from each different category will depend on how you view and categorize them. We need these various types of people and relationships in our lives to be able to begin to fulfill our God given assignment. In this book, most of our focus will be aimed at "Sonship". The relationship of a "son to a father."

FOUR STAGES OF RELATIONSHIPS

There are four progressive stages or levels on which people interact with potential fathers, and depending on what level you find yourself on, you will get the benefits that are attached to the price you must pay for that level of relationship. Yes, every relationship you have in life will cost you something and the deeper and the more meaningful the relationship, the higher the cost. Some friendships may cause you to have to leave something you are supposed to be doing to go and help a friend in need. This is what is sometimes referred to as the price of the relationship. The cost or the price is paid in terms of time, gifts, energy, resources, and sometimes vision or even life. These levels entail various relational entities such as the public (crowd), helpers (partners or staff), mentees (students, pupil) and sons (intimate, personal). There is no better level than any other. All levels of relationships are important.

The only time problematic issues may occur is when the definition of the relationship levels become blurred or crossed. This often occurs when one expects the crowd (level) to deliver what only a mentee (level) can give you. The same happens if you are operating on the mentee level, and in that specific relationship you expect from a father figure what only a son can do. Often someone may think people are not doing what is right just because one may have inappropriately categorized them and/or someone in an elevated role oversteps their boundaries and misplaces and/or abuses their authority. There is nothing more destructive than putting a partner in the place of a son or vice versa. Understanding the different levels will help you to know and understand your role, and how you need to behave. It is vital that relationships are defined early in the interaction so that there is less room for miscommunication and/or blurred lines that leave room for confusion and chaos in the relationships. Depending on the level of the relationship you are aiming for, this will help the person in the father's position easily distinguish and discern what their role should be, who is who, and what you should and can expect from them as the "father" and also how you are to act and/or respond toward him as the "son".

STAGE ONE

The first level of interaction to a potential father is the crowd, the masses or the public. When speaking in terms of business, this interaction would involve customers, everyone who interacts with a potential father in his talent area, and anyone who is consuming what is being produced. For example, since you are reading this book, you are consuming my product. If we were listening to a sermon in a church, we would be positioned in the role of a "customer".

This relational level is the first way most people will interact with what God has given them. There is no personal interaction at this level. It is more of an interaction with someone's gift or product and this is also similar to enjoying someone's fruit. The price at this level is the lowest. You may need to purchase a CD, a book, or pay to attend someone's speech; however, most of the time, there is no relational price to pay at this level. Most people will just stay at this level, and it is beneficial to you because most of the things you produce on this level are geared toward the masses. The public will eat the fruit you produce. The more consumers you have, the more valuable you are because your leadership is measured by the number of people you serve and the magnitude of your influence that you impart to them. This group is composed of consumers. They are associated to your past because they interact with what you have already produced. Some consumers may become very close to you, but you do not benefit from them except for their payment for your gift or services.

STAGE TWO

Some people among the masses will like and appreciate what you are doing, and will not want to just eat your fruits, but will rather want to help you to produce more fruits. They will either work alongside you for some compensation, such as an employee, or they will want to help you in the form of financial support to push you to produce more fruits. In churches and ministries these people often form relationships referred to as partnerships. These people will help you produce more fruits, but they are not submitted or committed to you. They do what they must do for you and after that they go back to their everyday lives. You cannot and should not expect loyalty beyond what you have agreed upon.

STAGE THREE

Some partners will want a deeper relationship and will go above and beyond helping you to produce more fruits to submit themselves to you and learn directly from you. They become mentees or students. You may even call them friends by the fact that they may know more about you on a personal level.

You multiply yourself into these people. They are your expansion. This is when we can really start talking about "sonship" at a lighter level or mentorship. Mentorship is a contract between a mentor and a mentee based on the need of the latter to learn from the former. This typically occurs when there is something that the mentor has that the mentee realizes they want or need. A mentor is someone who teaches, guides and lifts you up by the virtue of his or her experience and insight. They are typically farther ahead of you on the path; though, that doesn't always mean they're older! A mentor is someone with a head full of experience and heart full of generosity that brings those things together in your life (Definition by John Maxwell, International Leadership Coach). Sometimes mentorship starts when a mentor sees potential in you, and is willing to invest and partner with you for a season to help you grow and keep your thinking sharp and focused. Then the mentor makes himself/herself available for the relationship but the mentee must respond by pursuing the mentor and be willing to submit to the process of mentorship. Each mentor knows that his or her words make a difference in the mentee's life, but only when the mentee is willing to submit. That is why a mentor will normally close the relationship when they don't see commitment and submission.

Mentorships can have various levels, depending on the mentee's hunger and desire to learn and submit to the mentor. Mentorship is intentional on both parts. The mentor must be willing to teach you and the mentee must be seeking to learn. You can learn and even submit to someone you do not have a relationship with or have not met. It is easy to submit to one's words via a book, a video, or some form of audio media. I do not call this person a mentor, but just a teacher who impacted your life. All of us have access to long-distance teachers whom we may never meet in person. The list of available teachers is endless. In this age of digital experiences, there are more opportunities available for learning than ever before through books, magazine articles, and webinars. All you have to do is search for people who are succeeding in your area of interest, and you'll have a wealth of potential mentors at your disposal. Just make sure that what they say translates into actions or principles you can follow in your real life. After all, the point of any mentor is to help you take steps to get better! Mentorship is important for everyone's path to discovering and fulfilling one's life assignment because a mentor can give to you what they learned in 40 years in just 40 seconds. Most of the time, people do not fulfill their destiny because they tried to learn all they thought they needed by themselves while God was counting on them to learn from someone else so that they could can gain that person's time and experience in a matter of a short time. There is no such a thing as self-made individuals.

Some mentors are in our lives for only a short season; others are there for much longer. The length of the season is determined by what one needs to learn and what the mentor has and who the mentor is as a person. As I've said before, everyone needs some sort of mentorship in their life; and you must be intentional about finding the right mentor. The best way to find a mentor is to think of someone who is successful in a specific area that you are interested in growing and expanding. Start there and see how you can access that person's insights. Maybe it's through a blog, a book, or perhaps it's just a phone call away. You won't know until you start looking and asking.

STAGE FOUR

Some mentees will discover during their mentorship that they want to go even deeper in the relationship by submitting their personal authority, gifts, talents and their life to their mentor. This is when we can really start talking about "sonship". These students will take on their "father's" identity and desire to become just like him, or should I say become a different or modified prototype and prolongation of their father's DNA. This is a mentor's future—their next generation.

These mentees are the ones that will not only submit to their mentor but they will want to continue what their mentors do and even carry on their dreams and build their legacy alongside of them. These are the "sons". These are the ones that "fathers" want to invest in.

WHAT IS SONSHIP?

The dictionary defines "sonship" only as the relationship of a son to a father. However, I will define "sonship" as one's decision to learn, submit, and serve someone that they consider a "father" despite his or her weaknesses, and at the expense of their own comfort. Notice that I did add "her" because "sonship" and "fatherhood" in this context has nothing to do with gender because the word "Abba" in the Bible, from which we get the word "father", means "source and sustainer". A "father" is a source and a "son" is a resource. We are spiritual beings living in a physical body and there is no such thing as a female or male spirit. That is why there is no difference between women and men in the body of Christ.

The most definitive and important part of a relationship between "father and son" is the decision or the will because "sonship" goes beyond being natural born children. As a matter of fact, natural born children have to make a decision to become sons by submitting to their parents, and that decision is more important than their natural affiliation. Adoption takes place when someone decides in his heart and mind to "father" someone else. This type of relationship is more powerful than the natural affiliation because it does involve ones will to do so. Just imagine and receive the idea that God, the Father of all creation who is our natural source by creation and infinite design, desires and longs that we have this unique type of personal and intimate relationship with Him; He as our Father and we as His sons. He designed this ultimately magnificent, intimate design of a relationship with Him based on adoption. In the book of Romans 8:15, it says: "For you did not receive the spirit of slavery leading again to fear, but you received the Spirit of adoption, by whom we cry, 'Abba, Father'". Here we are introduced to this distinct, intricate, and definitively designed relationship. The verse above emphatically teaches us that even though we in this natural realm are the children of God by creation. We are only allowed to call Him Abba or our source and sustainer by the spirit of adoption. This is because He wants us to be His sons by our own will. The word adoption, translated in English is derived from the Greek word "huiothesia". This word "huiothesia" was originally a legal technical term and defined as the adoption of a son with the full rights of inheritance of the "father". If we are talking about a legal adoption, then we also must go through the process of qualification.

CHAPTER 2

RECOGNITION

The first step of this process of "sonship" is the ability to be able to "recognize" the father figure. This is when you find someone that you want to learn from who has excelled to the degree and level that you aspire and would like to obtain. You begin this process by consuming whatever they have that is available to you. Be it their books, recordings, writings, conferences, etc., you realize that you want to learn whatever they know and you are ready and willing to invest your life to learn from this individual. Recognizing a "father figure" does not necessarily lead to the "sonship" relationship. Sometimes the person may only be a teacher to you. As Paul, one of the first century leaders of the church wrote in 1 Corinthians 4:15,

> *"Even if the church he formed may have ten thousand teachers in Christ, they have not more than one father: for in Christ Jesus he had given birth to them through the good news."*

Paul tells them that you can learn from many people but when it comes to "fathers" you don't have many in each area. Note that he made it clear that the "sonship" he was referring to was limited to "a relationship with Christ". The difference between the role of "father" and that of a teacher is that "sons" learn to submit and serve a "father" who will sort of give them his DNA or his identity, whereas a teacher gives you knowledge, but you do not necessarily submit to them as an individual, even though you may submit to the knowledge they impart to you; you do not serve teachers. One becomes like their "father" while they will only emulate their teachers. You will continue what your "father" started, but you learn from your teachers to be able to do what is yours. You still have to honor teachers as people who contributed in your advancement but you do not have to walk in their footsteps.

You receive from people according to what you recognize in them. The Bible calls it a "prophet's reward". Mathew 10:41 states, "Whoever welcomes a prophet as a prophet will receive a prophet's reward, and whoever welcomes a righteous person as a righteous person, will receive a righteous person's reward."

Some of the people in the town of Jerusalem did not recognize Jesus as the envoy from God; the representative of God for them; and in turn, they could not and did not receive the miracles He had for them. So, it is the same way for us today. You must first be able to recognize the importance of receiving those who God sends into your life as "fathers" so that you are able to receive from them what God has given to them that is yours because if you don't recognize them as "fathers", you will prevent yourself from receiving from them what is yours!

The law or the principle of "recognition" is one of the most important laws in the bible. The "recognition" I am referring to here goes beyond just what our eyes or natural senses can perceive. It is a divine connection. It is when you encounter a person and you know without a doubt that this person has been sent into your life to take you to the next level. True "recognition" must be derived from a spiritual revelation more so than a physical or emotional sense of recognition. As a matter of fact, it is this same principle of recognition that one uses to choose a life partner, a husband or a wife. This is what the Bible calls to give names. When Adam was created, he was alone or all in one. So, he was not the final "creature" that God wanted. That is why God said in Genesis 2:18: "It is not good that the man should be alone; I will make him a help mate for him." God said that it is not good or perfect that man stay in that state. As a result, God went on to create for Adam a helper so that they both could fulfill God's assignment to dominate the earth together. What I find amazing though is that in the next verse, God did not create Eve right away. Instead, He first created animals out of the ground. God's purpose in doing so was to test Adam and find out what names Adam would give to these animals. Note that in the Hebrew culture the name given to a thing equals its destiny.

So, in other words God wanted to see if Adam would "recognize" anything in any of the animals that would cause him to believe that the animal was "a helper to himself". This is confirmed in the statement of the man after the animal-naming process in Genesis 20:2, "so, the man gave names to all the livestock, the birds in the sky and all the wild animals. But for Adam no suitable helper was found."

Adam said that he did not find a helper in any of the animals that corresponded totally to him. Let me explain something here: animals are just like humans when you consider their natural physiology as they are made from the same material, the soil of the earth. Therefore, if Adam the man was looking at the physical aspects of the animals, he was going to choose an animal as a helper, thinking that it would be suitable to him. This is what God wanted to find out, to see if man was more conscious of his earthly being or spiritual being. Adam passed the first test, which was to find out if he would identify with any animal as suitable helper for himself. When Adam did not, he passed the test. God then caused him to go into a deep sleep, at which time He created Eve from Adam's rib. When Adam saw Eve for the first time in Genesis 2:23, he said, "This is now bone of my bones and flesh of my flesh; she shall be called 'woman,' for she was taken out of man."

Adam recognized "in the woman" the "inside of himself". He "recognized" the bone of his bone, before he did the outside, the flesh of his flesh. He recognized his wife not on an "outside physical basis" which could have led him to choose an animal but he recognized her on a deeper level. He "recognized" that there was something "within her" that was just like him. Adam immediately connected with the woman on a higher level, a spiritual level.

Our blood cells are manufactured in the bones (hematopoiesis). Life is in the blood. So Adam "recognized" more than just the physical appearance of his helper. He could instantaneously connect with her spirit man. Many people choose the wrong partner because they limit their "recognition" to what they physically see with their eyes. To marry an animal is to choose someone who suits you physically, but who does not have the inner being that will suit your purpose and life assignment. This person may be a very devoted believer but it will end in a catastrophe because the person may have what you need from the outside point of view, but their inner being will never help you fulfill your purpose. This person was not designed to do so. So, be sure to name everyone that comes your way according to what you "recognize" in them and you will have the bone of your bones and not only the flesh of your flesh. When you "recognize" a "father figure" on a purely physical or emotional level that relationship will not stand the test of time. It will collapse at some point because only what is based on the Word or revelation from God will stand the test of time and last forever. You benefit from a father figure when you submit to them and their instructions, corrections and so on.

Submission is proportional to the level of "recognition" and you will not recognize someone just because you felt something, saw something or thought something of them. This is where many people miss it. They won't submit because of a revelation of who the person is in their life, but instead they will only want to submit to someone when their flesh and/or emotions desire to do so. Sometimes people will only submit to you when they are in agreement with you. In some instances, we can determine it was not a true act of submission nor was it based on proper "recognition", and whatever you will do on this basis will not last. There are instances when someone submits to you only because they are in agreement with you. In such cases, we can conclude that there was not an act of true submission, and that false act of submission will fail as well. There were Jews who had believed in Jesus but stopped when he told them something that was against their emotional and carnal thinking and they left him because their level of "recognition" was based on their emotions and not on what they received from God (John 6:53-68). The apostles told Jesus that they couldn't go anywhere else because they knew that He is their source of life!

The Apostles had recognized and known Jesus on a deeper level and not just with their physical senses. Jesus would check in from time to time and test them to show how deep their "recognition" of him really was, if they truly had a revelation of who He truly is. Once, when Jesus asked His disciples who do they say He is, Peter stated that He is "Christ". Jesus then told Peter that even though Peter had "recognized" that He, Jesus, is the Christ, the Son of the living God, not of blood nor of flesh, did not come from Peter, but that it was revealed to him by The Father in Heaven. In Matthew 16:17, Jesus replied, "Blessed are you, Simon son of Jonah, for this was not revealed to you by flesh and blood, but by my Father in heaven." Submission or abandonment is only by faith; by hearing the word of God. If your submission is not based on a revelation that you have, you will quit when tests come your way! Many people are submitted not because they are really committed, but because it is convenient. They will even abandon many things in order to submit, until something happens that threatens their comfort or their plans, and then they will show their true color. Never trust anyone who has not been tested! I have witnessed many people put trust into others and lose all they had built because they trusted someone before the testing time was over, and failed as a result—but by then it was too late and the collateral loses were great!

God does not look for capacity, gifts, or ability. He looks for faithfulness. Who can find a faithful person? Proverbs 20:6 indicates that "Most men will proclaim everyone his own goodness: but a faithful man who can find?" Being faithful is key to receive what God has for you. Your ability to submit to what God will tell you will depend on your ability to submit to fathers. How can you submit to a God you do not see if you cannot submit to a father that you can easily interact with? Many people are dedicated and will be willing to pay a price to be with you but they will leave you the minute you contradict them. Judas betrayed Jesus because He did not agree with him about the woman who poured the perfume on Jesus feet (Mark 14:1-10). Judas thought that the woman should have given them the money instead. As an accountant and from his standpoint, Judas may have been correct in his assessment (John 12:3-4) but he could not handle being contradicted by Jesus. Dedicated people are useful but abandoned ones are essential for your success (we will explore abandonment in further detail in chapter 6). You can build a family, an organization, a ministry, or a business with dedicated people, but true success only comes when you find abandoned people to work with you Moses was so abandoned to the vision God gave him to take His people to the promised land that he was willing to lose his place in the book of God instead of having a big name at the expense of God's vision (Exodus 32:31-32). Now this is abandonment. This kind of abandonment can only occur when there is a correct recognition based on what God told you. When you submit or abandon yourself to someone because you recognize them as being God sent into your life, you are trusting God and not the father figure and this will not only give you peace of mind but it will cause God to step in if the father figure is out alignment from God's will for your life.

ABANDONMENT PRECEDES ELEVATION.

CHAPTER 3

FOLLOWING

When you recognize someone as having something you need to fulfill your purpose, you must pursue him or her. You must follow the person and invest into that relationship if you want to benefit from the relationship. Every vision God gives you will require preparation, because when you receive the vision you need to be ready to fulfill it. That is why in every vision or instruction God gives you, it will include the people you will need to get connected to so that they can help you fulfill that assignment; but you must be willing to follow these individuals until you have received all they have for you. A good example of this principle is Mary receiving her vision to conceive the savior, Jesus. Mary asked the angel in Luke 1:34 how the vision would be fulfilled, and the Angel gave her the answer in two parts.

First the Holy Spirit would overshadow her. The Holy Spirit must always be the source of your vision. And the second part of the answer is found in Luke 1:36, "And look, your relative Elizabeth has also become pregnant with a son in her old age although she was called barren, she is now in her sixth month!" The Angel informed Mary who the person that had the key to her preparation was - it was Elizabeth. Every vision has an Elizabeth, a "who" that will help you. It is very important to discover who your Elizabeth is. Note that Mary did not decide for herself who she was to learn from or who her role model would be. The choice was made before she even knew about the assignment. Who is an Elizabeth? Elizabeth is a person who is already doing what you are called to do and this person is generally ahead of you on the path to fulfill their assignment. Additionally, this person has been pre-selected to prepare you to become who God has created you to be. Elizabeth was pregnant with a miracle baby just as Mary was, since her encounter with the Holy Spirit, but Elizabeth was already in her sixth month of pregnancy. She had already experienced what Mary was about to go through. Not only physically with morning sickness, nausea, body transformations, *et cetera*, but also emotionally. Elizabeth conceived and was carrying a baby at a very old age, past the menopause stage. Elizabeth was old in age and was far along in her years of barrenness. Can you imagine how Elizabeth must have been the subject of ridicule and gossip in her neighborhood? To manifest your vision, you will need someone who can tell you that what you are going through will pass and that you will be victorious in the end. Can you imagine what test Mary was going to endure? Not only was she single, pregnant, unwed, husbandless, but her child was conceived by faith–an immaculate conception. Who else could have understood her plight, except someone who was carrying almost the exact same vision? The fact that Mary had an example of what God did with Elizabeth would make Mary's situation and assignment much easier to receive and fulfill.

After the Angel explained to Mary about what Elizabeth was experiencing, Mary was able to surrender and accept the vision she was receiving. What I want us to focus on is the fact that after Mary accepted the message or the vision, she acted quickly and went straight to Elizabeth as we read in Luke 1:39-40, "In those days Mary got up and went hurriedly into the hill country, to a town of Judah, and entered Zechariah's house and greeted Elizabeth." It is important to follow closely the instruction imparted to you and build a relationship with the people God shows you that have what you need to fulfill your vision.

Take note of the fact that the Angel made sure to emphasize in verse 36 that Elizabeth was one of Mary's relatives. This implies a relationship and a connection; it is much more than just a teacher and a student. It is someone that you know well and can relate to. The following information is important to comprehend. You must know and understand that everyone is born to be a leader. I know this statement is problematic and may be somewhat difficult for many people to grasp now. Most people will ask: If everyone is a leader, then who will be followers? Everyone is born to be a leader, but the type of leadership we are talking about here is not over people, as many may define the term. Leadership in this context does not mean only leading people [even if eventually you can lead them], but the essence of this aspect of leadership that we are discussing has little to do with leading people. Leadership is the capacity to see or to capture a better future for humankind and to accept the process of paying the price to bring this better future into reality. Everyone was created and designed to lead and to master something and to turn a current situation or circumstance into a solution for his/her generation. You were created to lead in an area where you are gifted. However, you will not become the leader or the solution you were born to be, if you are not willing to follow someone first who is ahead of you in your area of talent. This period of following, submitting, and serving someone else will be a time of preparation and it will not only help you to refine your gifts, but mostly it will build your inherent character and remove what could be a hindrance to the fulfillment of your vision.

Many people will not live up to their full potential not only because they did not discover their purpose and/or vision, but because they did not want to submit to the process of preparation and testing. Can you imagine being admitted to a hospital and being operated on by a surgeon who was not properly trained and tested? Nobody wants that, agreed? That is why even Jesus had to undergo a period of 30 years of preparation and testing. Therefore "following" is imperative on your journey to fulfill the assignment that you have on this earth.

Bishop T.D. Jakes once said something that has stayed on my mind. He said that God is not really interested in us reaching our destination, but that He is more interested in the things we learn along the way. Sometimes the process or the journey is more important than the destination; it is very important for the final destination.

Jesus spent thirty 30 years with his family learning the family business and getting ready for His assignment that lasted only three and a half years. Maybe it was because He fully submitted to the preparation period so much so that he did not need as much time to finish his assignment and died saying that all was done. "It is finished." We should learn from Jesus and get it down deep in our heart and spirit if we want to "finish" our assignment just as well. During this 30-year period, Jesus was not leading. He was following people who did not have more power than Him or a bigger assignment than His. Actually, following someone has nothing to do with them being bigger than you. It is about people being authorized by God to assist you in becoming who you are meant to be.

Going back to Mary and Elizabeth, we see in Luke 1:56 that Mary stayed with Elizabeth about three months and then she returned to her home. Mary knew that she got all she needed from Elizabeth in those three months that she spent with her. The assignment Elizabeth had in Mary's life was fulfilled and then Mary went back home. Some people are assigned to your life for a specific period of time, not for your whole life. That is why it is very important to recognize "who is who" and "how long" you are supposed to follow the person. Since some people do not understand this principle, they stay attached to people even when their time with them is over. This has nothing to do with not being grateful; it is just the fact that your time with the person is over. The person has fulfilled their purpose in your life and has been a blessing to you and you have received all that they could give you. And if you have been faithful with what you have received from them, then you are ready to move on to the next level. However, I must warn you there are some, especially in this generation, that tend to short-circuit the period of following and training for the sake of not wanting to submit, or just because they do not agree with their authority in their lives. We will deal with this in the coming chapters.

Before continuing, I must say that it is crucial that your assignment is not finished until it has reached fullness in God's time. Just as Jesus knew the Father's business at the age of twelve, it was not time for that assignment yet. He had another eighteen years to serve and submit to his "assigned" earthly father. Jesus recognized that his preparation was not over and He needed to stay with Joseph, and submit to his nurturing while waiting for the right time to start openly His assignment. You will sometimes need to go from one mentor to another. When your "following" period to one father figure is done, you are not necessarily ready to go and fulfill your assignment. You may need to switch from one individual to another one, but you must be transferred properly.

King Saul understood the importance of "sonship". He understood "sonship" so much so, that when David had just killed the giant Goliath, Saul did not want to know anything else about him other than whose son he was. Saul somehow associated David's exploit of killing a giant with the fact that he must have been a "son" of somebody powerful. We can read in 1 Samuel 17:55-58,

> *"And when Saul saw David going out against the Philistine, he said to Abner, the captain of the army, Abner, whose son is this young man? And Abner said, on your life, O king, I have no idea. And the king said, make search and see whose son this young man is. And when David was coming back after the destruction of the Philistine, Abner took him to Saul, with the head of the Philistine in his hand. And Saul said to him, Young man, whose son are you? And David said, I am the son of your servant Jesse of Bethlehem."*

Saul would ask the same question three times about David until he got an answer. There is something else that I want us to understand about Saul and David's relationship, as well as the fact that when Saul wanted David to be under him, he had to ask permission of David's "father" to allow David to stay with Saul. As we read in 1 Samuel

16:22, Saul said to Jesse, 'Let David now stand before me, for he has found favor in my sight." Saul was a king and could have done what he wanted, but he understood that when it comes to the relationship of "sonship" everything must be done properly.

Even when Moses discovered that his time had come to go and deliver God's people and he had received a clear vision and instructions from God to go, he first had to get the go ahead from Jethro, his father in law who was his covering at the time that he was called. Exodus 4:18 says, "Then Moses departed and returned to Jethro his father-in-law and said to him, 'Please, let me go, that I may return to my brethren who are in Egypt, and see if they are still alive.' And Jethro said to Moses, 'Go in peace.'" This is very important to understand because if you dishonor a "father" just because you have found someone else to submit to, or because you are going to fulfill your own assignment, it will not last. Only a "father" can transfer you to a new "father". You cannot just decide to jump from one "father" to another. I remember the year I was appointed as a Trustee of the International Third World Leaders Association (ITWLA), founded by Dr. Myles Munroe - this was a result of me understanding this principle.

When I met Dr. Munroe, I knew he was going to play a role in my future, but what I did not know at the time was that you do not just decide to submit to someone else without being sent by the one who is covering you at the moment. Then, when I realized that I needed to do things correctly, I went to my Pastor and told him that I would not be going to the Bahamas for the Global Leadership Summit organized by ITWLA as I used to, unless he sent me there and thought that it would be beneficial to his ministry for the future. In the previous years, I simply told him that I would be going to the Bahamas; but this time, it is not just to inform him with information, but that the final decision was in his hands. He realized the importance of the decision he was about to make, and asked me for a timeframe to think about it before getting back to me. He is a very wise man. The next morning, he came back and told me to go, even if he was not fully aware of what it was all about. This time my "father" sent me to the conference, and at the end of the conference, I was invited to the organization trustee board meeting and was appointed as a junior trustee. Other friends who were with me did not get that privilege of being appointed as trustees, even though they were with me in the board meeting. I realized afterwards that the difference between us was that this time I was properly "sent by my father". Many times Sons are sent to their destinies by being transferred from one father to another "father"!

IF YOU ARE NOT SUBMITTED TO NO ONE,
YOU CANNOT SUBMIT TO ANYONE.

CHAPTER 4

SUBMISSION

The next level in a relationship is when you want to personally submit to the father figure in a mentorship. This is an intentional, informal transmission of knowledge, social, capital and psychosocial support perceived by the recipient in regards to personal or professional development. Mentoring entails informal communication and is usually face-to-face. Most of the time, mentoring is done by observation. Leadership is put into action for a sustained period of time, as an action between the mentor, who is perceived to have greater relevant knowledge, wisdom, or experience, and the mentee (protégé) who is eager and willing to learn and to submit. At this stage, we can't really talk about sonship; it is more of an advanced and personalized form of learning. When mentees have learned all they need, they graduate and are released into their respective destinies.

You cannot learn from someone you are not willing to obey; many people miss a lot from their mentors because they don't pay attention on the minor instruction. Sometimes a mentor will tell you to do things that may look small in your eyes, but when you don't cooperate, you are sending a message that you are not ready for mentorship. I remember one day, I was on a mentorship trip with Dr. Myles Munroe, and we were in Toronto, Ontario, Canada, which is a six to seven-hour drive from my hometown. After Dr. Munroe finished a whole day packed with general and private sessions at around 8pm, I hugged him goodbye and he told me these few words: "I will be in Boston after tomorrow." He did not tell me anything else. He jumped into the car with the team and they headed to the airport. For most people, that information would just be to inform me of where he would be, but as a mentee and someone who was willing to follow and learn all I could, I knew that it was an invitation for deeper mentoring time with him. I did not know where he was going to be in Boston, so I had to be very determined to learn from him to be able to make it to wherever he would be. I contacted the mentorship program office that night for his itinerary. Fortunately, we did have access to this kind of information within the program. The response from the office just stated that he would be at Harvard Medical School and that was it. I had to drive back home for seven hours the next morning, leave my car at home, and jump on a bus for nine more hours to be in Boston the next morning – without knowing anyone in Boston. I did not have enough time to make arrangements. I just knew deep inside that I had to be there. I was not sure if I could have access to the sessions, as it was not an open conference; but I was going to figure it out once I arrived.

What surprised me is that at 7:00 A.M. that morning, when I arrived at the bus station in downtown Boston, I received a phone call and guess who was on the phone? Dr. Munroe himself! It took me a minute to pick it up because I did not recognize the number and it was the first time he had ever called me. I did not even know he had my phone number. Anyway, I responded and he asked me where I was and he gave me instructions on how to get where he was at that time. But wait a minute: how did he know I was in Boston? All he had said to me was that he would be in Boston, not that I should come or anything else. That is when I realized he was testing me to see if I was serious about my mentorship. Do not ever trust anyone you have not tested. Many people will want to learn from you, if it does not cost them anything; but don't trust them with your knowledge and/or your life experience, because they will not value it. This trip was unique not only because I got a chance to be present in the room where Dr. Munroe received the first standing ovation any speaker ever received from Harvard alumni, but also because it was just Dr. Munroe and his son Myles Munroe Jr. on this trip. So, I had a chance to spend a lot of learning time from him, and I even got to know his son on a more personal level. Since I was willing to pay a higher price and take a chance to go to a foreign country, to a city that I was not familiar with, I am the only mentee who saw Dr. Munroe teaching the leaders of Harvard University and challenging them with "Kingdom Leadership" to the point they gave him a standing ovation.

Mentorship must cost you so much that you value the experience and the information that you are learning. As you seek more knowledge, understanding, and insight while mostly building your character, you are also investing in yourself. Receive and accept the price it may cost you, and you will be trusted. You cannot be trusted if you do not pass the test of commitment. Trust is tested over a period of time, so it never ends—and the more tests you pass, the more trustworthy you become, and the more access you obtain. Never trust a person who is not submitted to anybody because submission is a sign of maturity and self-control. God will never give power to someone who is not submitted, or I should say that God will not authorize anyone to use power, if they are not submitted. Submission is the key to obtaining authority. Do you recall what the Centurion told Jesus in Mathew 8:9-19? He said,

> *"for I too am a man under authority, with soldiers under me. I say to this one, Go and he goes, and to another come and he comes, and to my slave do this and he does it. When Jesus heard this, He was amazed and said to those who followed Him, I tell you the truth, I have not found such faith in anyone in Israel!"*

As this man understood "submission and authority" he had a greater faith than anyone in Israel.

As a matter of fact, submission is impossible without faith. Submission is a decision you make to put yourself under someone's mission (submission). You need faith and trust in God first to recognize the mission of the person you are to submit to and second to recognize your own greatness and plan to put yourself under someone else; not because you are weak, but because you are so self-controlled that you can manage to submit. The Bible says that one who controls himself is greater than the one who controls a city! (Proverbs 16:12)

CHAPTER 5

ADOPTION

Some of the mentees find that their life assignment is linked to their mentor's assignment and do not want to be released, but rather want to take the relationship to the next level of becoming a son. Just like in the natural, the father makes the decision first to father you, before you as a son can even make any choice; it's the father's decision to adopt you as a son. You cannot become a son to someone who has not adopted you first. Sometimes, a potential son will show commitment and submission that will trigger the adoption, but a son cannot auto-proclaim such. Fathers always adopt first, but the relationship is not complete until the sons respond and accept to submit to the fathers. That is why in Malachi 4:6, it starts by bringing the hearts of the fathers to their sons first and then brings the hearts of the sons to their fathers.

Naturally, a father accepts his son a long time before the son can make any decision. As I told you, even biological children must be adopted by their parents. It is not merely enough to have physical children. At some point, you must accept them and take the responsibility to nurture and care for them. We see many abandoned children because their natural parents did not get to the point of "adopting" them. This is probably one of the greatest tragedies of this generation so much so that we can refer to it as a "fatherless generation".

I travel around the world, and I am always astonished to hear the stories of so many people who grow up without their fathers or of people who never had a "father figure" in their lives. Not because they made that choice, but because their progenitors did not want to make the decision of adoption. A father is not only a source but is also a SUSTAINER. God is our "Father" not only because He created all of us. He is also our "Father" because He is our source and at the same time He sustains all things by the power of His word. What you "source", you are supposed to sustain. Hundreds of babies are killed in their mother's wombs because their parents do not want to take on the responsibility of raising a child, and by default, the abortion kills the chance for the unborn child to become a solution in their generation. Abortion is not just killing a baby; it is also the extermination of a purpose, a destiny. It is also the theft of a solution to a generation that the baby was bringing into the world. All of this happens when the "father" (the physical source male or female) of that child does not want to take the responsibility to adopt them. It is the same for sons. A father can adopt you, but as a son, you must decide to submit and be a son.

Why is adoption necessary? As you learned earlier concerning "sonship", adoption is more important than just natural affiliation, because both the "father" and the "son" must exercise a will and therefore must make the decision to choose. Adoption is when a "father" chooses a "son" and is willing to develop, train, sustain, correct, cover, protect and eventually give him an inheritance. Once a "father" has decided to adopt a son, he must let the son accept and respond to that adoption. "Sons" respond by submitting and abandoning themselves to the "father". The level of this relationship will depend on how far the father and the son are both willing to go, and this will be tested over time. This principle is probably the reason why God placed a tree in the garden to check and see if Adam would accept the responsibility to submit to the sonship principle. The "tree of knowledge of good and evil" was not that the tree was of evil as some tend to think. Rather it was to have access to the decision-making tool by them, outside of the will of God. When God the Father, source and sustainer created humans, His intention was for them to depend on Him for direction and choices. You cannot make decisions, if you do not have access to the knowledge of good and evil. So, when Adam took the fruit, he was basically telling God that he did not want to submit to Him. It was not only an act of disobedience; it was a "REBELLION" against God. Adam was saying that he wanted to be his own boss. Adoption will always be tested along the way. Sometimes a "father" or "son" will make a mistake that will put you in a position that will make you want to cut them off; however, the more tests you pass successfully, the greater the benefit of the relationship. Since God has placed the relationship of "fathers to their sons" and vice versa to the highest rank, He will always test that relationship before He can take you to another level. We see these tests throughout David's life, the greatest king of Israel and King Saul's life.

Saul lost his kingship because of disobedience and failed to recognize David as a son. Saul's perspective was a son could only be by natural birth, never considering adoption. Therefore, he looked at David as a threat to Jonathan's inheritance. Contrary to his thoughts, God sent him one of the best "sons" but he failed to "recognize" him and "adopt" him. David was actually sent to strengthen King Saul's legacy, but because of his lack of "recognition and adoption", not only did Saul lose his kingship, he also lost his life and one of his sons (Jonathan) in battle. On the other hand, Jonathan recognized who David was to him! "A brother" and he protected David. Now you can see how understanding "sonship" is key to being connected and fulfilling your God-given destiny.

THE FATHER ADOPTS THE SON; THE SON'S RESPONSE IS ABANDONMENT.

CHAPTER 6

ABANDONMENT

Abandonment happens when an adopted son decides to totally submit and surrender his potential to the father. This is the ultimate level of sonship. Many people do not reach this level because they want to hold on to what they believe they have, or simply cannot accept the idea of surrendering themselves to someone's vision, when they have yet to fulfill their own. Jesus said in John 12:24, "That unless a grain of wheat falls into the earth and dies, it remains alone; but if it dies, it bears much fruit." This is the principle of abandonment. Unless you lie down, abandon and forget your vision for a period of time while you are serving someone else's vision, what you have will stay a vision; you will not see any fruit from it. Reaching this level of "abandonment" can be a very difficult task to achieve for most. Even more so, if someone has already been made aware of the magnitude of their own vision, they find it difficult to abandon, because they are dealing with the complexities of "discovering their own purpose".

Perhaps you are in the midst of struggling with the "why" you were born, the "what" you are supposed to do, and in the process of seeking the Holy Spirit regarding the "how" you are to fulfill your assignment, when – BAM – you are all of a sudden instructed to not only set your vision aside, but to "abandon" it completely and indefinitely, while you take all of your resources and time and do whatever it requires to help

71

make someone else's dream come to pass. It is while trying to sort it all out and meet the challenges of "abandonment" and its timing that it is also when it seems that "abandonment" become a trap as well, while trying to work it out.

According to this principle of "abandonment", trying to work it out in your own understanding would be the worst thing one could possibly do. A sincere act of "abandonment" is only possible after your own vision has been revealed to you. Here, we will gain a more definitive definition of the term "abandonment" as it relates to "sonship". I will show in this chapter that there is a distinct difference between the act of submission and this new area of "abandonment". Relatively speaking, the two terms seem to be the same in nature, but you will find that as similar as they seem to be, they are highly different. Let me explain.

Both acts, "submission and abandonment" require that a decision be made to put oneself under someone else; but abandonment entails yet another prerequisite that runs on an even deeper level than submission. The act of "abandonment" as it relates to this teaching on sonship embodies a sacrificial component. Most people will find that this level of submission can be achieved without any problem; that is, until the day they receive their own vision. It is important to remember that at the time that you receive your vision, it is not the time to start working out your vision. It is the time when you are to bury that vision so that it can germinate and grow bigger, stronger, and produce much fruit. I feel the need to be more concise here and lay it out clearer for you: What many people initially perceive as a vision is not a vision at all—not initially. In fact, what they have is only a picture in their mind—an image that is not yet a clear picture of what they must do. It is just an idea of what they want to do, but knowing what to do is not merely enough to be able to do what you want or know to do. You need more clarity on how to do what you want to do and when to do it. Some assignments are very specific as to the time at which they must be fulfilled, with whom you are to work, *et cetera*. All of this information will only be revealed to you once you first put your idea/vision into the ground and serve someone else and help them accomplish their vision. Many people leave their position prematurely, just because they have received the first revelation. I have seen many people abort their life's assignment because they started to push their babies well before the baby was ready to be delivered. Many people leave their home church to go start their own ministry just because they believe they are called to be pastors. Very often, they have truly been called to minister and pastor a flock. Nonetheless, they lack understanding of "how" to do so and fail and/or delay their success because they acted prematurely.

Let us move on to obtaining a better understanding of "abandonment" and its benefits. The examples of Jesus and his assigned earthly father, Joseph, are the manner in which I can best explain my point when it comes to abandonment. As we read in Luke 2:41-52,

"Now Jesus' parents went to Jerusalem every year for the feast of the Passover. When he was twelve years old, they went up according to custom. But when the feast was over, as they were returning home, Jesus stayed behind in Jerusalem. His parents did not know it, but (because they assumed that he was in their group of travelers) they went a day's journey. Then they began to look for him among their relatives and acquaintances. When they did not find him, they returned to Jerusalem to look for him. After three days, they found him in the temple courts, sitting among the teachers, listening to them and asking them questions. And all who heard Jesus were astonished at his understanding and his answers. When his parents saw him, they were overwhelmed. His mother said to him, 'Child, why have you treated us like this? Look, your father and I have been looking for you anxiously.' But he replied, 'Why were you looking for me? Didn't you know that I must be after my Father's businesses?' Yet his parents did not understand the remark he made to them. Then he went down with them and came to Nazareth, and submitted to them. But his mother kept all these things in her heart. And Jesus increased in wisdom and in stature, and in favor with God and with people.'"

First, we see that at that time Jesus was 12 years old. That was about the age when a child could begin to make decisions for him- or herself. Even in our culture today, it is at this age when you are considered as maturing from a little child to a teenager. It is also when one can or typically begin to "make decisions" as to whether they will continue to obey their parents or not. We cannot even begin to talk about submission much before this age level.

Submission is derived from the Greek word "hypotasso". Hypotasso is defined as: to be under, to obey, be subject. It is a Greek military term meaning "to arrange [troop divisions] in a military fashion under the command of a leader." In non-military use, it was a voluntary attitude of giving in, cooperating, assuming responsibility, and carrying a burden.

Once again, the word "submission" is a decision you make to put yourself under someone else's authority, not because the person is better than you or anything like that, but because it is the right thing to do and you are the one who must make that decision. No one can impose or force you into the acts of "submission or abandonment".

According to the above referenced scriptures, not only was Jesus at an age where He was considered mature enough to be able to make His own decisions, but He had also come to realize or He had a glimpse of what His life's assignment was. He "saw" that He was supposed to be after the Father's business. Jesus even knew that His assignment would be in the area of "teaching", that is why "He was sitting among teachers" when He made the statement that "He had to be about His Father's business." Note, even though Jesus is and was God in flesh at that age, He was not yet the one that should have been teaching at that time. Rather we see in the scripture that He was "asking questions and learning" when His parents found Him. When his parents came looking for Him, they did not have an understanding of who He was. I must interject here that it is okay for your father to "not recognize" what you are called to do. Remember that only God can reveal you to someone, including your own parents. Rest assured that if God does not "reveal you to your father", then you must trust and believe Him that He did not do so because it was not in your best interest. I have seen many people get offended because they were not recognized.

WHEN IT IS NOT YET YOUR TIME, GOD WILL PROTECT YOU FROM RECOGNITION.

What is even more amazing to me is that Jesus obeyed Joseph and Mary and "made a decision" to leave the temple, even though He had stated, "He had to be after His Heavenly Father's affairs." You cannot first submit to God, "The Heavenly Father" if you are not willing to submit to your earthly father (parents) that God put in charge over you—no matter how big your assignment may be. Jesus accepted and "abandoned" His own vision, temporarily, while letting it fall to the ground, dying to self for 18 years. The only thing we know about Him during that period of time is that He was submitted to His "assigned earthly father", Joseph, and learned Joseph's craft as a carpenter and submitted to His parents in their household—under their roof. It is evident that during that time He developed Himself, increasing in all aspects of His life. Jesus had it right at the age of twelve. He knew His assignment, His "purpose", that He was to teach and "be after God's affairs". What was not yet made clear to Him was the "how" of His assignment. His assignment was not exactly like what the teachers of His time were doing. They were in the temple and His assignment would be to go from place to place. Yet, because He knew the "what" and not the "how", He went to ask questions to the wrong people. Hold on, I know it may sound crazy, but I will explain to you what I mean.

Jesus was asking question to the teachers of His time, but the message He was supposed to teach was not even known to Him at that time. Only John the Baptist came with the message Jesus was supposed to teach and that was "The message of the Kingdom". When God shows you your "what", it is still too early to do anything about it, because most of what you need to finish or even to start your work is not yet in place. I am glad Jesus accepted to "abandon" his vision for that moment because He was not yet ready to save the world at the age of twelve. He would not have been able or empowered enough to resist the temptations of the Devil if He had disobeyed his parents and tried to start His mission at the immature, premature age of 12. The colossal benefit of the act of "abandonment" or "to put your vision on hold" while serving someone else's vision is that you increase in knowledge, wisdom, and stature. These are the foundation for the main attributes of a fine character and grants us favor with God and also with men.

CHAPTER 7

ACCESS

When a father sees an abandoned son, he will grant him access to his heart. This is when a son can really get to know and understand not only what is on the father's mind, but that which is in his heart as well. After the disciples of Jesus abandoned all to follow him, Jesus told them that they were no longer servants but they were now "friends" who have access to what is on his heart. John 15:15 states,

> *"No longer do I give you the name of servants; because a servant is without knowledge of what his master is doing: I give you the name of friends, because I have given you knowledge of all the things which my Father has said to me."*

Once you have gained access to the heart of a father, your attitude will determine if you are a friend, a son or still a servant! Note that Jesus said that He no longer called the disciples servants. However, that did not mean that they could no longer behave as such! Today, we have so many sons and daughters of God who prefer to be addressed as "servants" of God. Some people think that to be called a servant of God gives them a higher status. We will differentiate between "friends and sons" in the last part of the book, but for now, let's see what differentiates "sons from servants". Sonship is more of a disposition of your heart. Sonship is so much more than the things you do. Sonship is mostly manifested through submission, service or simply "being after" your father's business. There is a vast difference between sons and servants. Both the son and the servant will "serve" the father but the way in which they serve or the reason they serve will be different. Sons will use their access to the father to benefit their father's vision and those who have a servant mindset will use the same access for their own benefit. It is what you do with the access to the father's life that will determine who you are. Servants expect to be paid for their services, sons work to build their father's legacy. It is important to have the mindset of a son because only sons stay in the house forever and can have access to more and eventually inherit everything that is the "father's". When you serve with a servant mindset, you can stay for a time, but you will eventually leave or lose your access.

There is a story in the Bible that we all know about: the prodigal son who asked for his inheritance before it was time for him to receive it. Let me stress here that an inheritance you receive before the proper time will not be a blessing to you when the proper time comes (Proverbs 20:21). When the son lost everything, he came back to his senses and decided to return to his father. When he returned home, he not only wanted to be treated like a servant with limited access, but he also expected that his father would treat him as a servant. Contrary to what he thought or expected, his father restored him and had a party so that everyone could celebrate with him that his son was back. The father understood that his future was in the number of sons he had and because of that he was ready to forgive and completely restore his son. Now, I would like for us to focus on the attitude and/or the mindset of the other son who chose to stay home and serve the father. Luke 15:25-32,

> "Now the older son was in the field: and when he came near the house, the sounds of music and dancing came to his ears. And he sent for one of the servants, questioning him about what it might be. And he said to him, your brother has come; and your father has had the young ox put to death because he has come back safely. But he was angry and would not go in; and his father came out and made a request to him to come in. But he made answer and said to his father, See, all these years I

have been your servant, doing your orders in everything: and you never gave me even a young goat so that I might have a feast with my friends: But when this your son came, who has been wasting your property with bad women, you put to death the fat young ox for him. And he said to him, Son, you are with me at all times, and all I have is yours. But it was right to be glad and to have a feast; for this your brother, who was dead, is living again; he had gone away and has come back."

When the older son came home, instead of him rejoicing with everyone else, he chose to be angry to the point of staying outside with servants. He was angry and he felt that because of the years he had never left home and had served the father, he was due to be recognized by his father. He felt that he had never received any pay because his mindset was that of a servant. Even though the younger son had messed up and squandered his inheritance, his mindset was still better than that of the oldest son's mindset. He knew that he could go back to his father, but the older son did not even consider himself as a son. It is sad to see how many people lose their access to their father and all the father has because they have the attitude and mindset of a servant. Again, servants will serve you just for their own benefit. Have you ever heard someone in church complaining that he or she has been serving there for many years and they have not been recognized? That is a sign of someone who serves just to gain something out of their service. This is not sonship. When you think of the situation this way and feel so in your heart, you cannot and will not be trusted for very long. That is why John 8:35 reminds us that the servant does not go on living in the house forever, but the son does.

One day, Joseph, one of the ancestors of the Israelites, shifted his mindset to that of a servant's and was forgotten as a result. It would take him two years to correct himself, before he could be promoted. Joseph had a very good "sonship" mindset from the time he was at his father's house, where he was serving his father without question. When Joseph was sold to Potiphar, he kept his same attitude. He was even tested for sonship when Potiphar's wife wanted to sleep with him.

Joseph did not want to take advantage of that offer, at the expense of his master (Genesis 39:7-20). Let's be candid, if you are a servant and your boss' wife offers to sleep with you, which would seem to be an upgrade or a promotion of some sort, if your mindset is not right you want to take advantage. You must understand that Potiphar was not at home most of the time. His wife was the one who managed the household where Joseph was working while employed by Potiphar. Having an affair with Potiphar's wife would not only elevate Joseph to his master's level just because he would be sleeping in his master's bed. Having an affair with his master's wife would have been beneficial to Joseph in the way that he would be treated on a daily basis. Yet, because Joseph had the proper attitude, and because he knew he was not there solely for his own personal gain, he accepted the task before him and submitted to pay a huge price and go to jail. No matter what situation you find yourself in; once you have developed a sonship mindset, you will always have access to everything you need, even if you find yourself in the position of a slave.

EVEN IN A PLACE OF CONFUSION OR MISUNDERSTANDING, A SON SHOULD NEVER DEFAULT TO THE LESSER RELATIONSHIP THAT IS OF SERVANT'S MINDSET.

After a few times in prison, something happened to Joseph because the next time he served someone else, Joseph attempted to take personal advantage from his work, as we see in Genesis 40:14, when Joseph stated "but keep me in mind when things go well for you, and be good to me and say a good word for me to Pharaoh and get me out of this prison." Joseph had just explained a dream and this time he wanted to use his service for his benefit. It did not work out quite well because for two years, the person forgot him. God was waiting on perfect timing for Pharaoh's dream and for Joseph to realize his mistake of promoting himself. We know that Joseph did change his attitude at that time because later a situation occurred that made Joseph have to go before Pharaoh, and serve him by interpreting a dream that no one else was able to explain. In that instance, Joseph did not try to speak for himself. He did not try to take advantage of his work situation. As a matter of fact, he asked Pharaoh to find someone else who could do the work even though it was his idea. He was no longer trying to be the center of attention. By now, he had gained back his "sonship spirit", and this time God was able to promote him. When you submit to a father with a right mindset, you do not need to promote yourself - God will do it for you. Genesis 41:33-40,

"And now let Pharaoh make search for a man of wisdom and good sense, and put him in authority over the land of Egypt. Let Pharaoh do this, and let him put overseers over the land of Egypt to put in store a fifth part of the produce of the land in the good years. And let them get together all the food in those good years and make a store of grain under Pharaoh's control for the use of the towns, and let them keep it. And let that food be kept in store for the land till the seven bad years, which are to come in Egypt; so that the land may not come to destruction through need of food. And this seemed good to Pharaoh and to all his servants. Then Pharaoh said to his servants, where may we get such a man as this, a man in whom is the spirit of God? And Pharaoh said to Joseph, seeing that God has made all this clear to you, there is no other man of such wisdom and good sense as you. You, then, are to be over my house, and all my people will be ruled by your word: only as king will I be greater than you."

When you have access, your attitude will either give you more (if you are a true son) or it will make you lose even the little access you had (if you have a servant attitude), and this will be tested—it is just a matter of time. Life is a succession of tests. You will always be tested before any promotion can take place; just as you cannot pass from one grade to another one without passing exams. Many sons are disqualified because they did not pass the tests of sonship, even though they may already have access. God will always test your faithfulness. Faithfulness in this context is defined as submission to someone's vision at the expense of your own comfort. God is looking for "faithful sons" and not servants (Proverbs 20:6). There is a difference between being faithful to someone and being faithful to what belongs to that person. Many people are faithful to their fathers but not faithful to their father's visions. Faithfulness can only come from the revelation that you have about your father's vision. Just as faith comes by hearing the Word of God, it is also impossible to possess faithfulness, if you did not hear from God. When God tests sons, He is testing the Word in them that He has given them. If you submit to anyone because of your own interests, you will not pass the tests. By the way, your faithfulness is tested in bad times. When there is something a father does that is contrary to what you would like, and your submission and abandonment are not based on what God told you, you will more than likely quit.

CHAPTER 8

COVERING

Once you have gained access to your father, you will begin to discover that he has flaws and this is a matter of when, not if. This is the time that your true essence of sonship is tested. Sonship is really tested when you discover your father's weaknesses. What do you do when you discover your father's weaknesses? As we saw at the beginning of this book, most of the time, your life assignment will involve things that are not in an area where you are your strongest. Sons are God's solution to this challenge. Sons are there to bridge the gap. For instance, Moses' assignment was to go and speak to Pharaoh concerning the children of Israel. He was not a gifted speaker; he even had a speech impediment. Can you imagine if his brother Aaron, who was a son figure to Moses, was publicly gossiping and complaining about Moses' inability to speak fluently and without stuttering? That was exactly why God had him beside his brother Moses. What Moses lacked and the area in which he was weak was what Aaron had in abundance, and that's what God was looking for in him. Sons are in the father's life to respond to their weaknesses. It is sad to see that many people do not see their father's weaknesses as a good opportunity to serve them even more.

When I think about this point of discovering your father's weakness, what first comes to my mind is Noah and his sons. In Genesis 9:21-23, we read

> *"When Noah drank some of the wine, he got drunk and uncovered himself inside his tent. Ham, the father of Canaan, saw his father's nakedness and told his two brothers who were outside. Shem and Japheth took the garment and placed it on their shoulders. Then they walked in backwards and covered up their father's nakedness. Their faces were turned the other way so they did not see their father's nakedness."*

This scripture shows us a father who made a big mistake and exposed himself under the influence of alcohol. What catches my attention is the fact that the first son who saw it was inside the tent with his father. As we saw previously, the more intimate you become to the father, the higher the chances that you discover what is wrong with him. The more access you gain, the more intense your tests of sonship become. Ham saw his father's nakedness and exposed it to his brothers who on the other hand decided to cover their father's nakedness—his weakness. They had the same experience as Ham, but their reactions were different. What happens when you discover your father's nakedness will determine your future. Nakedness is anything but what a father is proud of; it should not be on the market place for the whole world to see. True sons will always cover their father's nakedness because they know that this is where their blessings are.

Let us take a deeper look at Noah and his sons in Genesis 9.24-27, "When Noah awoke from his drunken stupor he learned what his youngest son had done to him. So, he said, "Cursed be Canaan! The lowest of slaves he will be to his brothers." Noah also said, "Worthy of praise is the Lord, the God of Shem! May Canaan be the slave of Shem! May God enlarge Japheth's territory and numbers! May he live in the tents of Shem and may Canaan be his slave!" All fathers have weaknesses and things to cover. We see that Noah's weakness became a source of blessing for the sons who chose to cover him and the same nakedness became a curse to the son who chose to expose his weakness. You will be cursed every time you expose your father's weaknesses because you are exposing what you are supposed to "fix". Every time God wants to bless or promote a son, He will create a need in his father's life. Son's destinies are always trapped into their father's needs. Father's get inspirations and sons transpire to make them a reality.

WHEN YOU DEVELOP THIS MINDSET, YOU WILL START SEEING OPPORTUNITIES INSTEAD OF SEEING PROBLEMS.

I remember one day when Dr. Munroe was teaching, he paused for minute or so and said he wished he could be able to touch and impact at least a million people every day with his teachings. When I heard that, I knew it was up to the sons to make it happen and I began to study ways to make that dream become a reality for him. Dr. Munroe traveled almost every day. He would be in America in the morning teaching at a breakfast, have an evening session in Nassau Bahamas, then would be in Europe the next morning teaching there, then on his way to Africa. The only possible way for him to be able to speak to that many people while he was traveling was to be able to "Live Stream" all his travels.

So, that is what I did. The point I want to make is that while studying and doing my research to make that happen, I discovered a passion I did not realize I had before. While serving my father, I tapped into a hidden ability that I did not know existed inside of me, the ability to broadcast the "Kingdom" message and make it available to the masses via the Internet. Not only had this journey with Dr. Munroe given me the opportunity to travel the world with him and his team. It had also provided me the privilege that granted me access and allowed me to witness first hand Dr. Munroe in different settings that I was not qualified to be in – like meeting heads of states and governments officials. Because I wanted to respond to his need, I was there with him. Observing, listening to sound counsel he was giving to everyone he encountered. Being privy to conversations and wisdom he was imparting to everyone he met. What I learned during those times that I was serving him and trying my best to make his dream(s) a reality surpasses by far what you can learn in the best schools on the planet. Out of my service to Dr. Munroe, I started a media consulting company, and am in the process of launching a web-based television network to make the "Kingdom" message available around the world. These ideas and abilities were trapped on the inside of me, and the only way they could come out was by covering or responding to a father's need. It all started by trying to help my father, what my father wanted, meeting my father's needs and not my own selfish desires. When Dr. Myles Munroe expressed his dream to speak to a million people daily, hundreds of other people were listening to the same teaching as me. By the way, at that time I was not present in the audience. I was at home watching him online while seated in my living room. I could help his dreams become reality because I understood the principles and keys I am sharing with you in this book. Always seek to find ways to cover your father's weaknesses or to respond to your father's needs, it will become a huge blessing to your life. Because of this, I was the only foreigner who was present in the Bahamian Parliament when Dr. Munroe was honored by the house of assembly of his native country. I have too many stories of what applying these principles birthed in my life and in the lives of so many other people around the world and throughout the history of humanity that pages of this book can handle. Often, I hear people complaining about what is wrong in their organizations, churches or even families and my first thought is always, why don't you try to do something about it? The reason you are uncomfortable about a specific topic or situation to the point of expressing it, is because you know what should be done to make it right. If you find a solution to what you are complaining about it will give you value. What you are complaining about is just an opportunity for you to shine. No one is promoted, celebrated or even paid for expressing problems. Only those who find solutions are rewarded, and you cannot complain about something and find the solution at the same time. Choose to correct the situations you encounter instead of complaining about them; doing this will increase your value.

A son will always increase his value in the eyes of a father based on the solutions he brings. Do you remember when the disciples were discussing among themselves about who is greater, or in other words who had more value? Jesus responded to them that the one who wanted to be great must serve. The key to your greatness is to respond to people's needs and this starts with you responding to your father's needs. Can you imagine for a second if David had complained about the inability of King Saul and his army to defeat Goliath? And trust me, he had enough reasons to do so! One could think he was justified if he complained if you do not understand "sonship". When you understand the principles of "sonship" you will understand that Goliath was there just to make David shine and to make him famous; not by pointing out the problem because everyone could see what the problem was but he became famous because he found a solution and killed Goliath for King Saul "his soon to be father" (1 Samuel 17). Most of the time, sons don't cover their fathers because they have become too familiar with them. Familiarity occurs when you start looking at the person instead of looking at the assignment and position of the person. Therefore, faithfulness is not toward the person, but to what belongs to the person.

THE MINUTE YOU BECOME TOO FAMILIAR
WITH YOUR FATHER, YOU WILL EXPOSE THEIR
WEAKNESSES INSTEAD OF COVERING THEM,
AND IT WILL CANCEL YOUR SONSHIP!

The closer you become to a father the more access you will have to his private life. The more access you have to your father's private life the more his weaknesses will be exposed and revealed to you. If you do not honor your father based on their position and/or their assignment you will become too familiar with their imperfections and you will not feel a need to cover his weaknesses! Familiarity is when you no longer have esteem for someone or look up to them because of their weaknesses that have been revealed to you. Once you come to know someone very well you will begin to learn a lot about them on a very personal level. You will also realize that they too have flaws like everyone else. You may also discover that they have some serious issues. While in the process of discovering these imperfections in your father and you may forget that "honoring a father" was a decision that you made to respect that person not based on their actions but based on their position in your life, you may make a shift in the relationship and move from the position of a son and become a friend.

FATHERS CAN AND SHOULD BE FRIENDLY, BUT THEY ARE NOT FRIENDS.

The minute you change your mindset from a son to a friend you remove yourself from the position of submission and become incapable of submitting to your father any longer. At that point you will begin to compete with your father and you cannot learn from someone you compete with. This is a very dangerous trap. How many churches have split up or have been destroyed because of this type of rifts? How many destinies have been hindered or halted completely because sons made the decision to expose their fathers instead of covering them? Covering someone does not mean that you ignore the situation or do not address what is wrong. There is a correct time and a proper way a true son can address his father's nakedness that can be beneficial to both.

Covering a father is first a state of mind. It begins with honor. Besides the number one task of a son is not to correct or reason with his father but to diligently seek and find solutions to his problems. Be like David, who told Saul who wanted to kill him that God would fix his problem. David knew that it was not up to him to do it. Sons do not judge their fathers. David was a man after God's heart, not because he was perfect, but because he understood these principles very well. Saul was one of the worst fathers in the Bible, but he was the one chosen for this period in David's development. Saul tried to kill David twice. Even though he was unsuccessful both times, he did not stop there. When those two attempts failed, he continued to go after David with his whole army behind him. Even though David had two opportunities to kill Saul during that time, he did not do it because he understood that sons don't judge fathers. As a son, you may have good reasons to judge your father. You may even want to pay him back for his wrongdoing, but if you do so you will not get to experience your greatness. I am telling you there is no wrong that a father can do to you that is worth forsaking your destiny trying to correct him and his shortcomings. Instead of exposing a father, bring him before God and trust Him to deal with your father in the right way. He did it for David. He will do it for you.

The other thing is that by exposing your father's mistakes you are likely to make the exact same mistakes. According to Galatians 6.1, "Brothers and sisters, if a person is discovered in some sin, you who are spiritual restore such a person in a spirit of gentleness, and pay close attention to yourselves, so that you are not tempted too." You can only avoid the same mistake when you cover it, not when you expose it.

When it comes to fathers, mentors, and teachers - whatever you do not like talk to God about it and whatever you do like, tell people about it!!!

CHAPTER 9

VALUE

When you cover your father's weaknesses or respond to his needs, you become valuable to him. He can trust you with more. God blesses sons through their father's words. These must come from a merry heart, though. It is when you quench a father's thirst that his heart can bless you. Isaac wanted to bless his son, but he knew that the only way he could truly transfer the blessing was if the son did something that would touch his heart (Genesis 27:4). Even when you are dealing with a bad father, this principle will work. David needed Saul who was the King to bless him so that he could inherit the "Kingdom of Israel". God knows how important a father's blessing is, that is why He allowed Saul to fall into David's hands. However, because David saved Saul's life, his heart was full of gratitude and he gave him the nation. Twice David spared Saul's life and twice he blessed him. 1 Samuel 24:20 says, "now look, I realize that you will in fact be king and that the kingdom of Israel will be established in your hand." Then, in 1 Samuel 26:25 Saul replied to David, "May you be rewarded, my son David! You will without question be successful!" So, David went on his way and Saul returned to his place. David was anointed King, but that was never going to happen unless David stayed in proper relationship with Saul, the King, so he could bless him and God could give him the nation. When you understand this principle, you will get all God has prepared for you. Looking from another angle at what David had to endure from Saul, we will conclude that it was all a set up for David to be blessed because God trusted his heart. God knew David understood sonship. He will not touch the one chosen and equipped to open doors for him, which is why He allowed Saul to do what he did. I wonder what God had in mind when He allowed what you went through or are still going through to transpire. A sonship mindset will allow you to take advantage of all the benefits of a son. This is a very important principle. Value your work. The value anyone will see in you depends on the need of the one you are serving. Many sons lose their place because they think that they are not valuable. You will be valuable or recognized when your time is up, keep serving faithfully. God is protecting you, because if your assignment is bigger than your father's house, it won't recognize you. Jesus told Peter that nobody can recognize who you really are, neither by flesh, nor by blood. Only God can reveal you to people. And most of time, He will do so by allowing a need only you can respond to. So, if He has not done so it is in your best interest. Many people abort their vision by leaving the fathers before time because they are in the hidden period. Stay where you are planted and grow until you are too big to be ignored. If you want to receive anything from a father, look at his needs. God the Father had a vision to redeem mankind and God the Son had to pay the price of His life to bring that vision to pass. He redeemed humanity for God, which is why Jesus received the name above other names (Revelation 5:9).

ADVANTAGES OF SONSHIP

A SON GETS ACCESS TO WHAT HE DOESN'T QUALIFY FOR

Mephibosheth was asked to see the King of Israel not because he did anything good, not because of his accomplishments, but because he was the son of Jonathan (2 Sam 9:3-8). David was looking for someone that was still left from Saul's family so that he could extend God's kindness to him. He was looking for a son of Jonathan, the son of Saul, to do good things for. Mephibosheth came to David bowed low with his face towards the ground, and was wondering why he had been summoned and even afraid. Remember David had just taken Saul's place as the King of Israel after a long period being chased by Saul who wanted to kill him. Mephibosheth would have been one of the last people to be the guest of honor of the new King David. He told him to not be afraid because even if he was not qualified at that time to sit at that table, because of his father, his affiliation, his sonship, he would not only have access to the king's table but he would recover all of the family belongings.

Sometimes you may feel like you are not qualified for something, but God gave you someone in your life who worked hard to qualify you. Trust me I know what that feels like. One day I was speaking to a group of people and said, "I didn't come here because of who I am or my achievements. It is because these people saw me serving a father, one of my mentors." I was not qualified to speak at this gathering of senior leaders in any way, but because of the affiliation I had, I was invited. I had gained access to something I did not qualify for. Submission to a father will always give you access to what you personally do not qualify for. This is an important key because you need that type of advancement for you to be able to fulfill your life assignment. If you start by yourself, you are not going to finish the race because the purpose and the vision God gave you is too big and He never intended the journey to start at your level. That is why when Jesus came on scene, He went and found someone who was ahead of him in preaching repentance and the Kingdom of God.

Jesus understood the need to submit to John the Baptist because He recognized the message of John was the same as the one in His heart. John had spent his lifetime declaring this message and Jesus wanted to continue this in John's place. Jesus benefited from John's work and advancement. Sonship, or the submission to authority, has nothing to do with anointing. It has nothing to do with you having a bigger vision. It all has to do with whom God has created to prepare your way before you. Mary carried in her womb the Creator of the One who was in Elizabeth's womb to the point that when Mary went to her the baby recognized Him. I think John the Baptist had to bow down in the womb that is why his mom felt his movement so strong and was wondering what was going on with this baby (Luke 1:40-43). Elizabeth was ahead of Mary in her pregnancy. She was in her sixth month. It is not about how large or important your assignment is. It is about the person God has placed before you! You better submit. Most people do not want to submit to others because they think they know more than the one who they have been sent to submit to; and sometimes even the person you want to submit to, is not aware and does not understand much. John the Baptist said to Jesus that He was bigger than him and that he must be the one to submit Him. In turn, Jesus said that they had to fulfill all righteousness, which is "I must submit to you John. I need to have access to what I didn't work for" (Matthew 3:13-15). And we will see how Jesus had access to what He did not qualify for. Yes, even Jesus was not qualified for some things initially. Stay with me I will show you what I am saying.

A SON STARTS WHERE HIS FATHER STOPS

A son always starts where his father stopped. Therefore, sons will always go higher than their fathers. The last work of Elijah was the first work of Elisha. Do you remember "how" Elijah opened the water going to the other side of Jordan? Once Elisha recognized the limitations of his own coat, he took his off and picked up the mantle of his father and he opened the Jordan on his way back (2 Kings 2:8 and 2 Kings 2:14). When you submit to someone, you don't start from the bottom you start exactly where that person stopped. Therefore, when you must submit to someone who may be insane it is still worthy of you to do so because you will benefit from his work. Just wait patiently and submit until it is your time. God will keep an unrighteous king on the throne as it was in David's case because the one who is supposed to come after him will start where he ended up. Samuel had anointed David to be King; however, there was a space of preparation between the anointing and the appointing that had to be in David's life. That space is called process. If God had removed Saul before the right time David was going to have to work harder. God said, I am going to keep him there, because when David becomes King the nation will already be established. The system will already be in place. David didn't have to go back and set these things in place. God had already made a way. If you do not submit to the person placed in your life as a father figure you will not make it to the end because you will do extra work that you are not supposed to do and get tired along the way and this will result in you not finishing your task. That is why even if the person is doing some foolishness, close your mouth and submit. Wait until God thinks you are ready and the person will bring the business where it is supposed to be. John said that Jesus would be bigger than him because he was going to start where he finished. Even Jesus said that those who are coming after Him, those who believe in Him, they are going to do what He did but because they are coming after Him, they must go higher, because that is the principle. Peter started his first meeting with more than 3000 people. Jesus did not have that many followers at the beginning. In many places, you will not find a company that has been there for the last 100 years. Do you know why? It is because people do not understand these principles, when you do not submit to a father there is no continuity. Even if the father himself wants it, everything a father worked for dies with him because there are no qualified sons who could carry on what he was doing. Most people must work hard to do the work that has been done previously because there was no continuity.

Understanding sonship is critical and God wants us to get it right so that there is no cutoff. There must be continuity in the businesses that we are doing. I remember that I was invited to go and speak in Africa before I was even a speaker in my own local church in Canada, because the one I was submitted to was an international speaker. I had an invitation to go and speak in another nation, on another continent before I even spoke once in my local community, because that is how God works. Every time God sends you a mentor, a father, it is not about the mentor being nice to you; God is trying to set you up. If you don't understand that, you will blow it all away and have to do double the work.

A SON GETS A VISION FROM HIS FATHER

A son gets his vision from his father. When you submit and serve a father you will receive a piece of the vision that they did not finish and you start with it. This is important to understand because God does not start your purpose when you are born. Remember, He starts at least three to four generations ahead of you. Many people struggle to have a clear life vision because God never planned to give it to them directly, but through their fathers. Solomon got the vision to build the temple from David his father. Joshua got the vision to conquer and take the land of Canaan from Moses and the list goes on and on. This principle is true because The Lord is a generational God. Every time He speaks to an individual He is not talking to that person only but also to his loins, his seed in him. When you understand this principle, you will understand how important sonship is. No transfer of vision is possible without proper sonship, submission and service. King Solomon takes this point even further in Proverbs 30:17, "The eye that mocks at a father and despises obeying a mother the ravens of the valley will peck it out and the young vultures will eat it." Eyes being an instrument you use to see, he is saying that you will lose your vision if you mock your father and disobey your mother because your vision is trapped in them. God had planned to have the nation of Israel. When the time came to start the process, He went to Abraham and gave him the instructions but what God had in His mind was Jacob and His 12 sons would actually be the ones to build the nation He wanted. Can you imagine if Jacob did not want to submit to his father Isaac? He would never have gotten what he was created to do because his life assignment was trapped in his submission to his fathers. That is why we always say that He is the God of Abraham, Isaac and Jacob. I did not have a burden of correcting the leadership problem in third world nations until I submitted to someone who dedicated his life to correcting this problem. It is only when I submitted to Dr. Myles Munroe and joined ITWLA that I started to realize that I was born to connect the third world people to their destinies by exposing them to the true essence of leadership. I did not know what was inside of me. I had not even realized that it was a specific problem. It was only when I connected to Dr. Munroe's passion and vision, that it awakened something on the inside of me. What stirred up in me was dormant and could not come to life until I was exposed to a father's vision. When it happened, I realized that my whole life was orchestrated in a way that I would be able to bring a solution to this problem.

Can you imagine that I had to be born in a nation that lost more than a million of its citizens killed by their neighbors in only one hundred days in a genocide prepared by the government? I had to experience the worse type of leadership that anyone can experience because I was born to correct the leadership philosophy that caused the 1994 genocide against Tutsis in Rwanda. Genocide is a systematic extermination of a people based on how they were born. It may not necessarily be to physically kill them. It may be to shorten their potential and prevent them from becoming all they could be. I had to experience a physical extermination of human potential because I was born to make sure people would be connected to their true self and have tools to become all they were born to be. None of this was going to happen had I not submitted to the vision of a "father". Even if all the gifts, talents or even the skills I had acquired were there to fix this problem, I could have never imagined that my life would be where it is because of this assignment. Now I know it, because I was connected to my assignment by serving a father figure. That is why you do not receive your life's assignment by just focusing on the tools that are there to help you fulfill a vision you can only get from a father. I wonder how many people are trying to find their life's vision in vain just because they did not recognize those sent in their lives to birth in them the vision God has for them.

A SON GETS WHAT HE NEEDS FROM HIS FATHER

A son gets what he needs to start his vision from his father because if the father left you a portion of the vision, he would provide for it as well. When I think about this point, the number one confirmation that comes to my mind is the relationship between Solomon and his father David; an ancient King of Israel. David had a vision to bring the nations together and to conquer the neighboring nations that God had promise to give to Israel. David mastered that vision with excellence and at the end of his life a persistent idea came to his heart to build a temple for his Lord. When God gives you a dream, it is so real that if you do not pay close attention to it you will confuse it with a vision and you may think it is your responsibility to make it happen. What happened to David's heart was so real that he wanted to build the temple himself. He went to God to make sure he had to do it. As we saw previously, you must use wisdom in situations such as this because it would be easy to make a lot of mistakes if you do all that comes to your heart without asking God's guidance as to how things should be done according to His purpose. God told David that it was not up to him to fulfill this idea. He informed David that it was in fact a dream and instructed him that he was to pass the dream on to his son Solomon. The question you may be asking yourself is why had God already planned and prepared someone else to fulfill the dream if it was David's idea? It was because this was what God had prepared for Solomon but it was necessary to first pass through David just so he could prepare everything Solomon would need to fulfill this vision. We will discuss more on this subject later about how a father will pass on his vision to a son in the last chapter.

As David said in 1Chronicle 22:5,

"My son Solomon is just an inexperienced young man, and the temple to be built for the Lord must be especially magnificent so it will become famous and be considered splendid by all the nations. Therefore, I will make preparations for its construction."

So, David made extensive preparations before he died. Because David is the one who received the vision from God he was also the one who knew how big, magnificent and splendid the temple should have been designed. On the other hand, Solomon was the one who was about to receive the mandate to build the temple, he did not have much experience at the time to ensure that all of the necessary preparations to build the magnificent temple to the Lords specifications. Nor would he have enough time to prepare and educate himself as to how it would actually have to be built to meet God requirements. In other words, the one who receives the vision is the one who is going to prepare for it.

This next point is as important as the previous one. The vision you will have to fulfill your purpose must be received from a father. If by chance you were to receive a vision without first having a father figure in your life you will not be able to properly prepare for it because you will not be equipped to do so without proper the access that only comes from a father. David was the only one qualified to prepare for what he saw and he did it by not only collecting material things such as gold, silver, and skilled manpower but also by building relationships with the necessary people. Solomon had to be instructed by David to go and ask the king of Syria for certain things and to go get this and that. It is very important to understand sonship and understand your father's relationships; he is building them for you. Remember even Jesus Himself got what he wasn't qualified for; do you know where he got his first disciples? From John, the Baptist, the one He submitted to. At the beginning of His ministry no one knew Jesus. Nobody was just going to follow him when He first started out but they knew John and he had authority. Do you remember in John 2.11 when Jesus changed water into wine? The Bible says that his disciples believed in Him. Wait a minute! This means that His disciples had not believed in

Him before then? They were already his disciples but he had not done anything prior to turning water into wine to cause them to believe in Him! Why then were they his disciples following Him? Let's move on. We are about to find out where he got them. This may be a good place to start explaining just how Jesus was submitted to John because I know this may cause some theological issue if not explained in much detail.

We can see beginning in Matthew 3:13 when Jesus came and said that it was important for Him to submit to John so that they could fulfill all the righteousness. As a matter of fact, in the book of Luke 20:2 when the religious authority of that time came and were questioning Jesus about who gave Him authority to do what He was doing, note that they never asked Him where He got His power from. Power is not the most important thing but it is the authority to use that power. Only a father can authorize you. Jesus responded to them in a parable, when He asked them if they recognized John's authority by asking if John's baptism was from heaven or human origin. He began with a question first because the response He was going to give them would not make a difference if they did not first recognize John. We must first understand what baptism represented in the time Jesus walked the earth to fully understand the meaning of these terms. Baptism was not invented by John nor was it a religious activity. All the master teachers who had schools of thought had some sort of baptismal ceremony for those who wanted to show publicly that they had joined their school and submitted to their teachings. Jesus coming to be baptized by John was His public display of submitting to John's teachings and philosophy. That is why John was arguing with Jesus. John had a revelation of who Jesus was and He thought, I am the one that should be joining your school and not the reverse. During that point of time Jesus had not yet established any school of thought. At the end of a master teacher's life, he would leave the school in the hands of his best student. Jesus joined the "School of the Kingdom" that John was preaching. What Jesus was saying to them was if you don't recognize my mentor you are just wasting my time.

Perhaps Jesus was thinking, "Do they recognize the one I am about to tell them that I get my authority from?" It is stated that they discussed it among themselves but could not respond. They did not know for sure if John's assignment to baptize was heavenly or not. Then Jesus said that He would not tell them from which authority He was doing these things because they would not believe him anyway. He must have thought something like, "If you do not legitimize my authority why should I waste my time answering you?" So, Jesus submitted to John by accepting to be baptized by him. The following day John was there with two of his disciples. He had a lot of students as he had worked long enough to be qualified to have students. When John saw Jesus he told his disciples "look the Lamb of God!" (John 1:35) When they heard, Him saying this, the two disciples started to follow Jesus. Those two disciples were Andrew and John who would become the most influential disciples of Jesus. You may be wondering how Andrew was influential as there is no book written about him. Are you asking yourself what did he do that would make me refer to him in that manner? When you read the scripture, you will find that Andrew had one of the most important tasks on Jesus's team. He was "the connector".

The first thing Andrew did after He met Jesus was to go out and find his brother Simon to tell him all he knew about Jesus. At this point, Jesus was not yet qualified to have disciples. Nobody had recognized Him for Who He was. Not yet. Jesus had not done anything personally but because John had pointed Him out in front of the crowd and said He was the One. As we discussed earlier doing so was an indication that John was handing his school and his students over to Jesus. That is why John said he would have to decrease so that Jesus could increase (John 3.25-30). The disciples of John who trusted their master followed Jesus just because of the words of John. Peter would not have followed Jesus he had not been referred to him by his brother, Andrew. When you start to work on your vision and because you will need a lot of people to fulfill it the first person you will need is a "connector". God will always start by giving you an "Andrew" and most of the time you will get him from your father's connections. We may not know many things about Andrew but this one thing is the most important thing in Jesus's ministry. You probably want to know why I make that statement, right? The answer is based on the fact of this next question. Who was it that would inherit the leadership of the church after Jesus's time was finished? Yes, it was Peter but between him and Jesus there had to be an "Andrew".

A SON INHERITS STANDARDS FROM HIS FATHER

A son will get his standards from his father. One of the major problems we are facing today is that this generation does not have standards because there are no relationships between sons and fathers. Proverbs 22:28, reminds us to not remove landmarks that were set by our fathers. The word landmark in this scripture is the word boundary. Our fathers set boundaries, they set limits as well as standards we are to honor not only because they set them, but also for our safety. It is something we measure other things against so we can know what to do and what not to do. Fathers will sometimes tell you "don't do this", "don't touch that" because they have knowledge of what works and what does not work. They are setting limits in your life. When you do not a have a father, you will experiment with so many things unnecessarily. You can spend so much time trying to figure out what is good or bad/right or wrong. The time you spend trying things can be wasted if you do not have a standard set before you. Standards are not put in place to limit you but to protect your time, energy and potential. God is always mindful of these things; therefore, you are not designed to do things by yourself without a father's input.

Dr. Munroe once told me that sometimes we learn from people the things that we are not to do more than learning from them things that we are to do, and he was very right. Sometimes what you learn from fathers are things to avoid. God can send you to submit to someone so you can learn what you are not to do. You may find yourself in a situation where you are even questioning God if you do not understand this principle. You may feel as though God does not see the wrong that your father is doing, but what God is more interested in is that you are aware of what the wrong actions can cause in someone's life and vision so that you do not make the same mistakes in your life. It is possible for God to allow you to be exposed to and witness some serious foolishness in someone's life that He is trying to protect you from and prevent you from going down the same path. David learned from Saul what to avoid more than anything else. We can see God telling sons in Ezekiel 20:18-19 not to follow the practices of their fathers. Here He is using the landmarks and the wrong doings of their fathers to warn them that they are not to do what they are witnessing their fathers doing.

So, how are sons expected to avoid making the same wrong decisions that they see the fathers making if the sons do not have the opportunity to witness the father's wrong doing in action? How can they be equipped with the knowledge and wisdom to make the correct choices without the example of the father's mistakes? Why would God speak to them in this way? How can this verse be applied to someone who has no father or a father figure in their life? What if the son has never seen a father or does not even have a healthy view of a father-son relationship in their life? What if a son does not know how his father is conducting himself because the father is absent or does not spend time with his son(s); therefore, the son has no valid example of how the father is walking out his life daily? Standards are the lines used to measure both good and bad, right and wrong, and sons can only obtain these standards from fathers.

A son gains experience without making many mistakes. He can gain experience without making many mistakes of his own if he has a father in his life to guide him in the right direction. This point is very similar to the previous one because if you are submitted to your father, you are going to see things in his life that may be contrary to the good that he is teaching you. You will see that a father can and will make mistakes, but the son is to learn from his father's mistakes and not to repeat them. A father may lose moneymaking investments, but he will talk to his son regarding the matter and instruct his son to learn from his mistakes and to not make the same mistakes as he did.

Dr. Munroe was always mindful of having his mentees with him so he could expose them to all he was doing, so that they could gain firsthand experience. I remember being on a trip with him where he was teaching a group of the government officials at the presidential palace in East Africa. After the session, he called me and one other mentee I was with to the side to make sure that we completely understood how to deal with government's leaders. A good father will expose his sons to what he is doing so that they can learn by observation. Sons on their side have the responsibility to be hungry enough so that the father is motivated enough to desire to teach more and more and add to their experiences. This principle will stop sons from making the same mistakes and prevent many catastrophes. Every time you make a mistake it will cost you something. Even though God's Word teaches us that once we repent, He is quick to forgive us, this does not remove consequences that can be generated by the mistake.

Not only will you waste the time you are spending making the mistake but also the time used to correct the mistake. Don't forget to include the energy you are spending as well. A son will be protected from this waste when the father's experience is transferred to him.

A SON IS SENT TO HIS DESTINY BY HIS FATHER

The book of Psalms 127:4 tells us that, "sons born in someone's youth are like arrows in a warrior's hand." Arrows in a warrior's hand are there to be shot or sent away. Warriors shoot on targets; and just as these arrows are in his hands, sons will be sent to their destinies by their fathers. God will always give you a father figure who is going to send you where you need to be. Your destiny will always be trapped in someone else's hands and it is by serving that person that you will find yourself in a situation that will open your own destiny. Most of the time the father does not even do that on purpose, but when God sees that you are faithful to what belongs to someone else, He will make sure that your faithfulness is rewarded.

Throughout the Bible, where people discovered and fulfilled their purposes, you will always find a father figure sending them to the place of appointment with their destinies. What made David known to Israel as a mighty warrior and opened the door to him to become the King? Isn't it when he killed Goliath? How did David find himself in front of Goliath? His father sent him to the battlefield to check on his brothers, and while he was there, the situation to reveal him presented itself (1 Samuel 17:17). As a matter of fact, the name "Goliath" is derived from a root word that means to reveal oneself, to be put on display, or to be made known. Goliath was the situation to reveal David – to display who he was and what he was capable of doing. Remember that he was already a mighty warrior, but when David killed the bear and the lion (1 Samuel 17:34-36), he was by himself in the bush with just the flock of his father. Nobody knew how mighty he was until exposed by Goliath's death.

Preparation is performed in secret. Once God sees that your preparation time is completed and He is ready to reveal you to the world, He will put you in front of a Goliath. Each person will have a Goliath in his life, and only a father will send him in front of his Goliath. Some people may think that Joseph made a mistake when he shared his dream with his family because his brothers tried to kill him. But, when you look closely, you will find that in the process of trying to kill Joseph his brothers actually sent him to the place where his vision was going to be fulfilled. Instead of killing the dreamer, they helped him to fulfill his dream. You may be wondering what this story has to do with sonship. What I want to point out is the fact that Joseph was sent to his brothers by his father. It is because he was obedient to his father's instruction that he found himself in Egypt, and that is where his destiny was (Genesis 37:13).

How did Moses discover the clarity of his life assignment? It is when he met God at the burning bush, right? He found himself at the burning bush while he was looking after his father-in-law's cattle. He was taking good care of his father's business, and that is how he found his own life's assignment. We can also mention Saul again here. Saul was the first King of Israel. He met Samuel, the prophet who anointed him king when he was looking for the lost donkeys of his father. These situations were just a set up for him to be sent into his destiny by serving his father's need. It had nothing to do with the donkeys as they had already been found, and now everyone was worried about Saul while he was being made the king of Israel (1 Samuel 9:15-20). Because we have different stages in our lives of fulfilling our destinies, every time you need to pass to another level, you must be sent by a father figure to meet your specific type of Goliath situation.

I understood this principle when I first met Dr. Myles Munroe. I was in Nassau, Bahamas, his hometown, attending one of his annual conferences on leadership. Then, one night after the conference I met a couple from the United States of America. We were having an interesting discussion, and they became even more interested in me and my friend Norbert when they learned we were genocide survivors. The next morning when we reached the lobby of the hotel where the conference was being held, they were waiting for us. They just came out and announced that they wanted to be my American parents. They implied that they wanted to sort of adopt me if I wanted them to. I did not think much about it at the time. I agreed to their request but without really realizing what that meant. Only a few seconds passed after our verbal agreement adoption when we saw Dr. Myles Munroe walking towards us. Now, more than 300 people attend these conferences and most of them have something they want to discuss with Dr. Munroe, so he was always surrounded by crowds of people.

He really enjoyed spending time with people. But, what I did not know was that my then mum, Leslie, had attended school at Oral Roberts University with Dr. Munroe when they were younger. They were very close friends with my adopted papa Graham also. So, when Dr. Munroe saw them, he changed his path and came our way. I stood there amazed and a bit nervous, as they were very excited explaining to him how I had spent hours and hours listening to all his material on YouTube and had almost memorized all his words. He laughed as I imagine he'd heard these words so many times. Before I knew it, I was invited to join them in the board meeting that they were having right afterwards, and for the first time I was in an ITWLA Trustees board meeting.

When I went back to my hotel room that night, I asked the Holy Spirit to explain to me all that the adoption thing was about, and He told me that Dr. Munroe was going to bring me into my destiny and that I needed a father figure to connect me to him. That was a few years before I started traveling with Dr. Munroe. He explained to me that night that adoption is better/greater than natural birth because in the case of an adoption you choose to be a son, and that was a starting point of my journey. The point I am making here is that my relationship with Dr. Munroe started because a father, who had adopted me just a few seconds before, introduced me to him. This principle is so strong that it will work even if the father's intentions are to harm you, as long as you obey, submit, and serve with a right mindset. The principles of sonship are God's way of connecting you to your destiny no matter what the father wants or does not want to do. As a son, you just have to apply these principles, and they will work for you. Nobody including your father can stop what God has planned for you. The only person who can do that is you because God will never impose on you what you do not want to do. The easiest way to short cut your destiny is to not apply God's principles. Principles are not set to limit you or to burden you in any way, but rather, they are there to help you go quickly and surely.

Coming back to Joseph, whose story can be found in Genesis 37-40. Joseph did not want to sleep with the wife of his boss, Potiphar, who was a father figure for him; and the fact that he did not want to dishonor a type of father, led him into prison. That is also where he was connected to the situation that made him the ruler of Egypt, and he fulfilled God's plan for his life. It is important to understand that it is not really the father who sends you into your destiny but rather the act of being faithful to what belongs to your father that connects you to your destiny.

One of the fascinating applications of this principle is the story of David, the greatest king of Israel. The thing that made David's reign so special was a strong army. David's army was so strong that during his time, Israel conquered all the surrounding nations, to the point that when Solomon, his son took over, there were no more battles to fight. Now, have you ever asked yourself the question of where David got his army? David met the group of people who were going to become the mighty men of David while running from his father Saul who tried to kill him, and he chose to flee instead of resisting him. It was not the number of opportunities to kill Saul that David lacked.

Now, if Saul had not attempted to kill David, do you know what David was going to inherit? Saul's army. Saul's army was so bad that they could not even protect Saul (1 Samuel 26:15). David was able to get too close to Saul twice while Saul's army was running after David to kill or capture him. This was not an army that would have made David's reign powerful. God knew that Saul's army was not what he had planned for David, and He used the evil that Saul wanted for David and turned it into good. As long as David submitted and did what was right, all Saul did was turned it into David's advantage. Even if your father wants to kill you, if your attitude is right, God will use your submission to benefit you. The only loser will be the father. If Saul understood this and had accepted David – helped him – his name was going to be greater. When you submit to a father, it does not matter what he is doing because God will keep His word, and He said that He would conform everything to the good for those who love Him and are called according to his purpose.

A SON DOES NOT HAVE TO DEFEND HIMSELF

One of the benefits of sons is the fact that a father will always be your cover or your back up. When you submit to a father, your problems become his problems, and a father is in a better position to defend you than you would have done by yourself. This is true for the times when a son messes up or he does something that he should have not done. First of all, whenever you mess up, you lose the right to be heard, and you will need someone in the position of authority to defend you so that you can be restored. We see so many people making the mistake to try to comeback from shortcomings on their own and by themselves. Therefore, they will never recover completely the lost trust or authority because of their mistake. But, when you have a father, he can restore you back. When Peter denied Jesus publicly, he lost his place of authority among the disciples; but when Jesus rose again, the angel that met some of the disciples and reminded them of the appointment with Jesus on His behalf was the one who defended and restored Peter back to his position by telling the other disciples to specifically remind Peter where they had to meet (Mark 16:7). Peter would not have been able to join the group again without Jesus showing them that He still trusted him and counted on him. When a father decides to restore you, nobody will argue even if they are not agreeing with the decision.

I hope you remember the parable we saw previously of the prodigal son; he went and misused his father's money, and when he came back, his brother was not happy about it. But, because it was the father who had not only received him back into the family but also restored him to his position of a son with access represented by the ring, nobody could do anything about it including the big brother. Everyone will make a few mistakes on the way to fulfill their destiny. If you do not have a father whom you can run to, to get restored and be brought back, chances are that when you mess up it will be impossible for you to get the trust back because most of the time a lost trust is never restored. I had an experience with my colleagues one day in an executive board meeting, and I had done some of the things on the instructions of the CEO of the company that I work with and people were attacking what I did. I was so quiet because the CEO was present and he jumped in and defended me without even saying that he was the one who gave me the instructions. What amazed me the most was that he came to me after the meeting and thanked me for not saying anything. Because I understood how being under authority works, I did not try to defend myself and he was so happy with how I handled it and allowed him to cover me. In life, the most secure place to be is under authority because you benefit first hand from that authority. You take advantage of the authority without having it personally.

ONLY A SON CAN HAVE SONS

Maybe the most important benefit of sonship is the fact that only sons can have sons. The way God created the universe is everything reproduces after its own kind. You cannot expect an orange tree to produce lemons. That's why if you are not a good son, you will not produce good sons, and this will cause you problems because you can only fully fulfill your life's purpose through your sons. Many people don't understand why they don't have in their organizations faithful people who help them to bring their massive visions to pass. If you did not sow into someone else's vision and submit as a son, do not expect anyone to do it for you. Sons are the ultimate blessing. It is no wonder why when God came to Abram and told him that he was going to reward him greatly, Abram's response was that he does not have a son. He asked how he could be blessed. I think he understood something very deep. Your blessing depends on your ability to reproduce yourself into sons, and He did not want to leave his inheritance to a servant (Genesis 15:1-3). This is exactly what God confirmed when He said in Deuteronomy 28:11 that, "The LORD will grant you abundant prosperity by multiplying the fruit of your womb, the young of your livestock and the crops of your ground--in the land he swore to your ancestors to give you." In other words, you can only get abundant prosperity when you have many sons, or according to God, you can only prosper abundantly when you have many sons. Sons will protect you against those who come against your interests as David reminds us in Psalms 127:5, "Happy is the man who has a good store of sons; he will not be put to shame, but they will support his cause against his haters." Many fathers kill their own sons, not necessarily by a physical death, but they curse them and destroy their legacy just because they have not been sons themselves. Sonship trains you to not act in rush because you are submitted. It teaches you to be patient and still, mostly in a situation when someone is doing something wrong. I am not saying that sonship prevents you from confronting what is wrong but you learn how to do things in a right way and at the proper time.

Let us look at some examples like in Genesis 9:21-25,

"Noah drank of the wine and became drunk and lay uncovered in his tent. And Ham, the father of Canaan, saw the nakedness of his father and told his two brothers outside. Then Shem and Japheth took a garment, laid it on both their shoulders, and walked backward and covered the nakedness of their father. Their faces were turned backward, and they did not see their father's nakedness. When Noah awoke from his wine and knew what his youngest son had done to him, he said, 'Cursed be Canaan; a servant of servants shall he be to his brothers.'"

Do you know, for example, why Noah did not curse his son who did expose his nakedness and cursed his great son instead? He understood this principle; you protect your sons no matter what they do, because this is where your abundance lays. Sons are very important because any vision God gives you will be bigger than you. Your vision will always require not only more than one individual, that is yourself, but also it will require more than one generation, and this is your sons. Moses could not have fulfilled his assignment without Aaron, who was a type of a son and an asset to him. But at the age of 40, Moses was not in a position to recognize his brother as a son until he himself became a son – submitted and served someone else. Remember Moses was first a prince – being served and not submitted to anyone, and you can only reproduce who you are! After a while, Moses understood the importance of protecting his sons, which is why when Aaron and Mariam did what was wrong and God wanted to kill them, Moses interceded for them. By the way, what Aaron and Miriam did was to violate the principles of sonship, did not honor Moses, and compared themselves to him probably because they were too familiar to him as most people become with their fathers, which will prevent them from honoring them (Numbers 12).

ONLY GOOD SONS PRODUCE GOOD SONS

Unfortunately, because many people expose their fathers, they will do the same with their sons, and the cycle continues. My hope is that this book will stop this destructive cycle and allow God to fulfill His plans in our generation.

CHAPTER 10
LEGACY

"Success without a successor is a failure." Dr. Myles Munroe

The dictionary defines legacy as something left or handed down by a predecessor, but I would like us to define it as a dream, a piece of vision, that a father passes on to the next generations to fulfill. Legacy is a very important stage of life. I love Dr. Myles Munroe's quote, "Success is not what happens when you are alive; it is what happens when you are gone." He was referring to the importance of legacy. Legacy is the most important piece of life when it comes to leadership. Legacy is what you will be remembered for. There are three stages you will need to master to have a successful life or to finish the assignment God has prepared for you. The first stage of life is preparation – the period when you are being prepared for your assignment. This is the stage of sonship when you serve and submit to fathers who will connect you to your life vision and assignment. The second stage of life is manifestation – the period when you are bringing to life, or manifesting, the vision you received.

The last stage of life is succession; in the last, but not the least, stage is when you are preparing your legacy by producing and equipping sons who will fulfill your dreams. Unfortunately, many people only focus on the second stage of manifestation and don't pass the tests of sonship nor prepare their legacy, which jeopardizes their chances to fulfill their destinies. They will not fulfill their purpose because they will miss the first portion of vision that you can only get from a father and because you can only reproduce after your kind. They don't have sons, so their dreams die with them. Therefore, God said that if the relationship between fathers and sons is not corrected, He has no other choice than to destroy the land. The destruction is built in if there is no passing on. What a tragedy!!! Life is not a marathon where you run as long as you can and try to cross the finish line by yourself, but life is a relay where you get a baton, run as fast as you can to finish your leg, and pass on the baton safely to the next runner, who will do the same so the whole team will finish the race! I hope this book will open your eyes so that your dreams won't be taken with you to the graveyard. One of the biggest mistakes in life is to leave your legacy in the hands of chance; to avoid this is to prepare the generations to come while you are still alive and strong enough to make sure that the baton is well passed to the next generation.

In many relay races, teams are disqualified because the baton is not properly handed to the next runner! I remember what happened to the U.S Olympic 4X100 meters men's team in the Rio 2016 Olympics that cost them the bronze medal; it was a baton not properly passed on. Unfortunately, this happens a lot in companies, churches, and family businesses, or even on the national level. Don't leave your legacy in the hands of a person you did not have time to father and test for sonship! We are going to see in this part of the book what the principles are to follow in order to prepare properly for your legacy and choose a successor, who will not only protect your vision but who will pass it to the next generations. This is critical because if the life vision you have is from God, it is bigger than your lifetime. Without proper succession, there will not be continuity in what you are doing, and this is a big problem because of the way God thinks and operates.

As we saw earlier, God thinks in generations. Every time He speaks to you, whatever He is telling or showing you is for your son's sons. Proverbs 13:20 says, "that a good man leaves an inheritance to his children's children." We know that God is not talking about the material inheritance, even if this can be included, but God is more interested in the vision. A good man leaves a vision that is big enough to be passed on to two generations. This can only be accomplished through Sonship. The task of the Holy Spirit when He comes in your life can be defined in Joel 2:28, "Afterwards, I will pour out my Spirit on all people, your son and daughters will prophesy, the old man will dream dreams, and the young man will see visions." This verse is showing us two different kinds of the revelations the Holy Spirit gives to different groups of people – a vision and a dream. The difference between a vision and a dream is that a dream is to be passed on to the next generations.

Abraham had a vision and a dream. God gave him a vision to have a son, but He had also told him he was going to build a nation; he never saw that nation because it was a dream. When God comes to a young man, He gives him a vision; and when He comes to an old man, He will give him a dream expecting that person to have sons to inherit the dream and turn it into a vision. When a dream is passed on to the next generation, it becomes a vision. Sons are incubators of their father's ideas; they develop them and materialize them.

FATHERS HAVE DREAMS, AND SONS MAKE THEM A REALITY.

A vision is what you are supposed to fulfill in your lifetime. God says that young men will see visions that He will give you depending on your age. Maybe I shouldn't say your age, but your stage, because in this context old and young do not have much to do with the age. Jesus was an old man at 33 years old, for example. He had a dream to change nations, but in His lifetime, he didn't touch the whole world. He only touched and impacted one group of people – the Jews. Changing nations didn't happen until the next generation of disciples. His dream had to wait until the third generation from Jesus. Paul, who was used by God to change nations, was not the first generation of disciples; there was Jesus, the apostles, and Paul. That is why the righteous are blessed to the third and the fourth generation. That is when real things start. When God comes to you and promises something – gives you a vision – He will only give you one piece to fulfill and another piece of the vision to pass on to the next generation, your sons; and the process continues through to the third and fourth generations. That is why it is very important to understand these principles.

God said in Malachi – the last verse of the Old Testament – that He will have to bring back fathers to the sons and sons to the fathers, or He will have no choice but to destroy the land. Destruction occurs because there is no continuity, and this is very important for the process of nation building because what God wants to be done is so big He has to use multiple generations without having to start again and again. He wants the generations to build on what previous ones have already done. By nature, a dream is just like a vision. When one receives it, if you do not pay attention, you will think that what you have in mind is what you must do.

FATHERS GET INSPIRATIONS, AND SONS TRANSPIRE TO MAKE THEM HAPPEN

When David had the idea to build the temple, it was so real to him that he thought he would be the one to do it. It also happened to Moses, whose vision was to deliver people from Egypt, but God's dream was to take them into the Promised Land as a nation. Moses even tried to negotiate with God to let him be the one to bring the people into the Promised Land because it was so real to him as if he was the one to do it. This is one of the traps of fathers. God showed Moses His dream so he could impart that dream to Joshua, who was the one called to take the children of Israel into the Promised Land. This is one of the reasons that many people do not prepare their sons to take over while they are still alive and make sure not only that the passing of the baton is done smoothly but that they are prepared with all the sons need to fulfill the vision they leave with them. It is critical to know when your vision is complete, so as to prepare and eventually pass on the baton. It is better to pass on the baton too soon than to do it too late. At least when you do it too soon you are still around to guide and correct your sons and make sure that they have the support they need when they begin.

One of the reasons I believe God admired David was the fact that he knew when it was time for him to hand the kingdom to Solomon. He was the only king of Israel that saw his successor on the throne (1 Kings 1:47-48). All the other kings where replaced when they died. David handed the baton while he was still alive. No wonder why He is the man after God's heart. Many times, in the bible the blessing or favor of God is attached to having children. This is because God is always thinking about legacy. No matter what you do – how good you can be – you cannot fulfill all God has prepared during your lifetime; the only way to continue and finish what God has for you is to reproduce yourself and have sons who will build your legacy. One of the promises God gave the children of Israel was that if they obeyed his laws, no barren woman or man would be found in their midst (Deuteronomy 7:14). They would have sons to carry on their dreams.

YOUR LIFE VISION IS NOT FULFILLED BY YOUR ACHIEVEMENT ONLY BUT ALSO BY ACTIONS OF THOSE YOU LEAVE BEHIND; THIS IS YOUR LEGACY.

Legacy is more important than one's achievement. Preparing a good legacy is living beyond your lifetime. Legacy allows you to live beyond your graveyard! Now that the importance of legacy is clear, let us see how one must prepare a solid legacy. Legacy is built by the collaboration of all your sons to achieve the vision you left them. The task of a father is to bring the sons together, to make sure that they understand that all of them are important to the vision, to build in them the sense of responsibility toward the vision, and to set the authority in place and make it known long before they die. I have seen many family businesses, organizations, and corporations that were left by their founders without a clear leadership in place. Then, what happens is that everyone is trying to fit in without any harmony, and it may cause problems that sometimes will kill the vision. The father must leave in place a successor who will be able to bring together his siblings and manage to motivate them enough to keep the vision alive. The objective of any father who wants to be successful is to not only have many sons, but also to make sure they are one, unified with a clear vision to achieve that is bigger than all of them individually. That is the only way your legacy will be built and your vision will live on! The last public prayer of Jesus was to ask for unity of those he was leaving behind (John 17:21). There is nothing that can stop your legacy more than the lack of unity of vision among those you leave behind. You cannot afford to have more than one vision in place at a time because that is what brings division.

Your legacy is built only when your vision lives on and survives to the third or fourth generations!!!! A righteous man leaves inheritance to the sons of his sons. A vision takes generally at least three generations to be developed enough to be viable! That is why wise fathers make sure to transfer their vision while they are still alive and strong enough to be able to guide their successors, monitor how their vision is executed, and make sure that it will be passed on. One of the things that will prevent division is to understand that only sons are qualified to carry on your legacy. As we saw above, Abraham was concerned by the fact that a servant was going to inherit from him, and he was right because only sons receive an inheritance. They are the ones who can continue your work because they have your DNA.

You can only leave your legacy in the hands of people you can fully trust. Never trust your future with an untested person. You can only trust those you trained yourself.

TRUST IS A RESULT OF TESTS OVER TIME.
TRUST ONLY THOSE YOU TRAINED YOURSELF.

God said that the prophet Elijah is the one He will send back to fix the problem of sonship because he proved to have understood how dreams work and how you choose your successor and make sure that your legacy is strong. When Elijah was tired, he thought his life assignment was over and he asked God to kill him (1 Kings 19:4). Because his vision was over, he did not have anything left to do, at least that is what he was thinking when he asked to be taken away. But an Angel came to him and asked him to eat because he still had a long way to go.

Let us see together what was next for him. God revealed Himself to Elijah and gave him instructions concerning the task he still had to accomplish. As we read in 1 Kings 19:15-16,

"And the Lord said to him, 'Go back on your way through the waste land to Damascus; and when you come there, put the holy oil on Hazael to make him king over Syria; And on Jehu, son of Nimshi, making him king over Israel; and on Elisha, the son of Shaphat of Abel-meholah, to be prophet in your place.'"

What intrigued me is that Elijah did not start by the first instruction given by God to anoint Hazael and make him king over Syria. He did not even go to the second instruction to anoint the King of Israel, but he went only to look for Elisha who was to succeed him.

At the beginning when I was reading this story, I thought that the prophet was becoming disobedient until I realized that he understood when you are tired and too old to run, what God gives you is a dream and all you must do is to start preparing your replacement and train them to fulfill your dream. When Elijah met Elisha, he did not tell him what God said. He did not anoint him right away in his place, but he took him on a series of tests to make sure that he was qualified to succeed him. Wait a minute, how can anyone picked by God himself be unqualified? Or, does God pick the one to succeed you? Let us see what happened to Moses when he found himself in the same situation as Elijah – when he was tired and could not handle the task given to him by God to the point of asking death for himself. As we read in the book of Numbers 11:14-15,

> *"I am not able by myself to take the weight of all these people, for it is more than my strength. If this is to be my fate, put me to death now in answer to my prayer, if I have grace in your eyes; and let me not see my shame."*

Both were tired and the response of God was the same in both cases. When you are tired and feel as if you can no longer to fulfill the assignment, it is a sign that you have reached the point to have sons who will help you; and from this time on, the focus should be to qualify and prepare them.

Let us continue by checking what both mighty men of God did respectively. God responded to Moses in Numbers 11:16-17,

> *"And the Lord said to Moses, 'Send for seventy of the responsible men of Israel, who are in your opinion men of weight and authority over the people; make them come to the Tent of meeting and be there with you. And I will come down and have a talk with you there: and I will take some of the spirit which is on you and put it on them, and they will take part of the weight of the people off you, so that you do not have to take it by yourself.'"*

God gave Moses the responsibility to qualify those he wanted to work with. It is always your responsibility to test those you want to leave your vision with.

What I want us to see is that when Moses got to the point of entering the Promised Land and he had to choose spies to go and check the country, he chose from the group he had brought to God, and who was supposed to have received his spirit. Let me stress that the spirit of Moses refers here to his vision, not any other kind of spirit because we saw that the spirit generates the vision. This being said, now my question is to how come only two people seemed to have really received Moses' vision and understanding of God's assignment? Because among twelve people sent by Moses to check on the land they were about to enter, only two of them gave an encouraging report as we can read in the book of Numbers 14. Caleb and Joshua did manifest the same spirit as Moses. What could have been the common factor that made a difference between Joshua and the rest of the group, to the point even God could not successfully transfer the spirit of Moses? The difference is that only Joshua submitted and served Moses as we can read in Numbers 11:28, "Then Joshua, the son of Nun, who had been Moses' servant from the time when he was a child, said, 'My lord Moses, let them be stopped.'" It is not possible to receive the vision of someone you did not submit to and serve. Even God Himself cannot override that principle because He can't violate His own words. You can only reap what you have sown. When Moses was tired, he looked for helpers, people who would carry the burden with him. He did choose the leaders of the people, but only Joshua submitted and served Moses; and that is the only one who managed to get it.

Many companies or organizations don't expand to their full potential because of this same issue. You can't build a sustainable organization if you are working with your friends or servants – people who love you but cannot fully submit to your vision. Even God can't manage to give them your spirit. Elijah did not want to experience the same thing as Moses, and he followed the principles everyone should follow to qualify sons who will inherit from him. The first thing Elijah did was to make himself available to Elisha and let him know that he was ready to have a relationship with him – what we could call to adopt him.

1 Kings 19:19 states, "So he went away from there and came across Elisha, the son of Shaphat, plowing with twelve yoke of oxen, he

himself walking with the twelfth; and Elijah went up to him and put his robe on him." The robe represented acceptance into the family, and it was Elijah's invitation and sign of adoption. But, what Elijah was looking for was more the response Elisha would give to his offer to be adopted by him.

Let us take a look at what was Elisha's response in 1 Kings 19:20,

"And letting the oxen be where they were, he came running after Elijah, and said, 'Only let me give a kiss to my father and mother, and then I will come after you.' But, he said to him, 'Go back again; for what have I done to you?'"

The response of Elisha was good to some extent, and as we saw previously, he recognized him and was ready to follow him and submit to him. But, what Elijah was looking for was abandonment, and this is critical because anyone who is not ready to abandon all he has and be willing to follow you and your vision, is not fit to succeed you. Elisha had some other priorities. He wanted to first say goodbye to his family and eventually he wanted to keep his business aside just in case. Do not trust someone who has a plan B. They will not build your legacy when tough times come, and trust me, challenging times will come. The person will go back to his other plans. Do you remember that Peter once asked Jesus what they would receive because they left everything behind to follow Jesus? This is the first step to choose a successor; the person must be willing to leave all they have behind to follow you. Elijah refused what Elisha was offering and sent him back. At some point, Elisha understood and decided to abandon himself completely.

As we see in 1 Kings 19:21, "And he went back, and took the oxen and put them to death, and cooking their flesh with the yokes of the oxen, he gave the people a feast. Then he got up and went after Elijah and became his servant." He went back and destroyed his business; forsook everything to the point he would not be tempted to go back. Now, this is total abandonment. And, only at this point did Elijah accept to take him under his wing because he has shown that he was sold out for the relationship and vision. Abandonment is the first test of qualification for succession.

Now, we could think that it was over. Elisha is now qualified because he abandoned all to follow Elijah, but that is not the case because you cannot trust someone who has not been tested over time; and that is what Elijah was going to do. He is going to take Elisha on a journey and this process takes time. This process took more than six years for Jack Welch – the former CEO of GE (General Electric), an American Fortune 500 multinational conglomerate corporation listed the fourth-largest company in the world by Forbes – to appoint Jeffrey Immelt as his successor. As some have said, "GE was the Super Bowl of CEO succession planning." It does take time, energy, effort and dedication from you to make sure that the one you choose is the right person. Your legacy is entirely into their hands.

Let us continue to see what you must be looking for in this person. According to the most successful succession plan of the Old Testament – and it was the same principles applied by Jesus - the first thing Elijah was looking for was to make sure that his successor has a son mindset and not a servant mindset. Servants will stay with you for a time but not forever. Someone can be committed and serve you for a long time, but if the person has a servant mindset, he will leave you when you go through hard times or when his interests with you cease. Do you remember in 1 King 19:2-3?

> *"Then Jezebel sent a servant to Elijah, saying, 'May the gods' punishment be on me if I do not make your life like the life of one of them by tomorrow about this time.' And he got up, fearing for his life, and went in flight, and came to Beer-Sheba in Judah, parting there from his servant."*

When Jezebel threatened Elijah, his servant left him because it was no more in his interest to stay. Look how those who submit to you react when everyone else is against you and when you go through hard times. A son will stay with you no matter what because he does not have anywhere else to go.

A son will stay even against your suggestions to leave you, but servants will leave. This was the difference between Ruth and Orpah when they were asked by Naomi to leave her as we can read in Ruth 1:8-18,

> "Naomi said to her two daughters-in-law, 'Listen to me! Each of you should return to your mother's home! May the Lord show you the same kind of devotion that you have shown to your deceased husbands and to me! May the Lord enable each of you to find security in the home of a new husband!' Then she kissed them goodbye and they wept loudly. But they said to her, 'No! We will return with you to your people.' But Naomi replied, 'Go back home, my daughters! There is no reason for you to return to Judah with me! I am no longer capable of giving birth to sons who might become your husbands! Go back home, my daughters! For I am too old to get married again, even if I thought that there was hope that I could get married tonight and conceive sons, surely you would not want to wait until they were old enough to marry! Surely you would not remain unmarried all that time! No, my daughters, you must not return with me. For my intense suffering is too much for you to bear. For the Lord is afflicting me!' Again, they wept loudly. Then Orpah kissed her mother-in-law goodbye, but Ruth clung tightly to her. So, Naomi said, 'Look, your sister-in-law is returning to her people and to her god. Follow your sister-in-law back home!' But Ruth replied, 'Stop urging me to abandon you! For wherever you go, I will go. Wherever you live, I will live. Your people will become my people, and your God will become my God. Wherever you die, I will die - and there I will be buried. May the Lord punish me severely if I do not keep my promise! Only death will be able to separate me from you!' When Naomi realized that Ruth was determined to go with her, she stopped trying to dissuade her. So, the two of them journeyed together until they arrived in Bethlehem."

You know, because Ruth was a true son, she is listed among very few women in the genealogy of Jesus.

So, Elijah is testing to see if Elisha is a true son or if he is just a regular servant. He tried to persuade him to stay behind while he is going somewhere else in 2 Kings 2:2, "Elijah told Elisha, 'Stay here, for the Lord has sent me to Bethel.' But Elisha said, 'As certainly as the

Lord lives and as you live, I will not leave you.'" And this happened several times, Elisha responding exactly the same. And something else popped up when other sons of the prophet, or other people who were being mentored by the prophet in what were called the school of prophets. Not only did they not want to follow Elijah because they knew he was going to leave and so they had no more interests in him but they tried to get Elisha to follow them and stop going with Elijah. 2 Kings 2:3 states, "Some members of the prophetic guild in Bethel came out to Elisha and said, 'Do you know that today the Lord is going to take your master from you?' He answered, 'Yes, I know. Be quiet.'" They did not want to follow Elijah because they considered him to be their master and not a father. You can leave one master for another one when it is more convenient for you, but you cannot leave a father for another one. And the test is even deeper when you consider the route the prophet Elijah was taking. He left Gilgal to Bethel, and then went to Jericho, heading to Jordan. This looks like he was going out of the Promised Land and that he was heading in the wrong direction. It looks like he is going back Egypt, and this is a huge thing for an Israelite. It is confirmed by the fact that 50 men of the sons of the prophets went with them until they reached the Jordan River, and they did not want to take a chance to cross it and decided to stand afar and watch Elijah and Elisha (2 Kings 2:7). Some people can start with you and pay a price for a while, until it becomes crazy to continue with you, and will decide to just look and support you from afar and not get fully involved in what you are doing. Do not trust these kinds of people with your vision. Only after they crossed the Jordan River is when Elisha was almost qualified to succeed Elijah because he stuck with him all the way and he was the only one who crossed the river.

I said almost qualified because we are now going to see what the final qualification is. 2 Kings 2:9 states, "When they had crossed over, Elijah said to Elisha, 'What can I do for you before I am taken away from you?' Elisha answered, 'May I receive a double portion of the prophetic spirit that energizes you." Elijah was now ready to give him whatever he wanted.

The last point before you even consider a person for succession is to check if he not only considers himself to be a son but also if he wants to be your successor with all the responsibility attached to it. Do not give to people what they did not ask for because they will not value it. Elisha confirmed both when he asked for a double portion. I have listened to a lot of teachings about double portion and some have even promised to give you a double anointing and so on, but I prefer to let the Bible explain itself.

The meaning of a double portion is not someone giving you double of what they have. It is not even possible for someone to give you more than they have, right? It is a sign that the one who receives it is your first-born son. A firstborn son was entitled to receive twice the inheritance of the father's other sons in addition to the right of succession, as we can read in the book of the law in Deuteronomy 21:17, "But he shall acknowledge the firstborn, the son of the unloved, by giving him a double portion of all that he has, for he is the first fruits of his strength." The right of the firstborn is his. It is one thing to be a first-born and another thing to want to be the successor.

We are going to see the last and final qualification before succeeding anyone. Elijah replied in 2 Kings 2:10, "And he said, 'you have made a hard request: still, if you see me when I am taken from you, you will get your desire; but if not, it will not be so.'" Note that the request is not hard on Elijah because he is not the one to do something to make it happen, but to Elisha. He must see Elijah while he is being taken. This means that the last and most important qualification is to be able to catch the vision and to see the same thing the father is seeing at the time to receive the baton. It does not matter how long someone stayed with you. He can be as qualified as you want, but if the person does not see what you see, do not leave him in charge of the family, organization, or business. The qualification is to be a son who loves you, is faithful, can see what you see for the future, and is willing to pay the price to make it happen. If your successor just loves you, he will manage and protect well what you have done and secure the continuity, which is already something good. But, love won't take your vision to the next phase, only faithfulness will do that.

Being faithful is to be willing to die for the vision!! When you love someone, you keep his commands and you keep his words, but only love is not enough for succession. Once you love the person, you must be faithful to what belongs to him. That is why Jesus asked Peter after he confirmed that he loves him to then take care of his sheep (John 21:16). The most important part of succession is to take care of the vision. Peter loved Jesus without a question, but at the beginning he did not really care about Jesus's assignment. He loved the man, but he was not faithful to His assignment! As a matter of fact, Peter loved Jesus so much that he did not want him to die for His assignment (Matthew 16:21-22).

Most of the people who love you may be a problem to your own assignment because they may try to prevent you from paying the necessary price to make it happen. The first century church leader, Paul, understood the key to sonship and legacy. That is why he asked Timothy, his son, to transfer what he has learned from him to sons only – those who are faithful so the vision can keep going. No wonder we still have his writings today. 2 Timothy 2:1-2, "You therefore, my son, be strong in the grace that is in Christ Jesus. The things which you have heard from me in the presence of many witnesses, entrust these to faithful men who will be able to teach others also."

Let me show you how loving someone without being faithful to what belongs to him can hinder his vision. When Moses was taking the children of Israel from Egypt to the promise land, he was the one everyone else was looking up to. Then, one-day other people in the congregation started prophesying, or started to get access to the spiritual realm. Joshua who was Moses's servant was so angry because for him they were taking Moses's spot! He could not understand that it was very good for the vision, may be not for Moses as an individual because he considered them to be his concurrence, and Moses had to rebuke him (Number 11:26-29). Of course, it is better to have a successor who loves you than the opposite because the one who does not love you will destroy all you have done. The one who just loves you will manage well what you have accomplished, but he will not be able to take it to the next level!

It takes someone who loves you but who also loves your vision as much as you do. They must be willing to die for it because that is the only life they have. Now, not so many sons will qualify here. I am talking here about the successor who will be coordinating what other sons are doing to build your legacy. All the sons build the legacy but only one can succeed you.

We talked about sons in opposition to servant, but I want to come back to a category of people we did not really talk about – friends. As we saw previously, friends are generally at the same level as you. We can add also that friends are a person who knows your heart and what your plans are, versus servants who do not necessarily know your heart. They may submit and even dedicate themselves to your vision, but if they have other visions, they will not abandon themselves to your vision. Friends are very good company for your present, but they are a big threat to your future if you do not understand well how to deal with them. A father must understand who are servants, friends, and sons. We have servants who do not necessary know what is on the heart of a father and friends who have access to his heart. Friends do not necessarily become sons. I would even say that they barely become one. Do not get me wrong, friends are very important to your destiny as well as servants. Friends are a very good source of support and strength, especially at the beginning of your journey. But, it is important to understand the nature of your relationship with them. The minute you understand who is who, you are in a better position to know how much access you give to them and mostly, what to expect from the person you are dealing with!

Let us take a look together at the difference between these three categories of people on your way to fulfill your Kingdom assignment – servant, friends, and sons. Friends are faithful to you, not necessarily to what belongs to you. That is why they can be dedicated, helping you to achieve what you are doing, they can even sacrifice a lot, but they are not going to abandon themselves for your vision. Friends do not really submit to you; they collaborate with you. They cannot fully submit because you are at the same level. Friends will support you, serve, and help you to achieve your goals as long as they agree with you, or as long as it does not conflict with their own things. What is most important to friends is your relationship to them and not really your vision, because friends have their own visions. Actually, they will work with you not because of your vision, but because of their own visions. The difference between servants and friends in this context is just that friends have access to what is on your mind. So, both servants and friends will not stay forever with you. Or, I should say that they will not stay forever with your vision. Only sons stay forever because they have no other vision than what you have. Friends take care of your person and family, but sons take care of your vision.

YOUR SONS ARE DEFINED BY HAVING NO OTHER VISION THAN YOUR VISION.

You will know how to classify people around you when you give them access to your heart. A son covers their father's weaknesses; friends try to correct their friend. Your friends will compare themselves to you. Miriam and Aaron are a very good example of friends. They had access to Moses' heart, they understood his vision, but because of their familiarity as his great brother and sister, they considered themselves equal to Moses as we can clearly see it in Numbers 12:1-2, "Then Miriam and Aaron spoke against Moses because of the Cushite woman he had married (for he had married an Ethiopian woman). They said, 'Has the Lord spoken only through

Moses? Has he not also spoken through us?' And the Lord heard it."
Their argument was that God speaks to them just as He does with
Moses.

When it comes to vision, there is no such thing as a vision given to
a group of people. A vision is always given to one individual who
shares it to the rest of the people and the visionary in this case is the
father. Another good example of a friend who served without being
faithful to the person's vision is Joab, David's nephew. Joab spent his
life as a dedicated soldier of David's army. He was his chief of staff.
We see so many times that he risked his own life for David, but when
you look closely, Joab was not submitted to David at all. He would
only do what was in his personal interest and he would only obey
David when he agreed with him. Many times, he did things that would
look good for David as a person but were very harmful for his
kingship and future. Joab cooperated with David in the murder of
Uriah, Bathsheba's husband (2 Samuel 11:14-25). He bore an
important part, successfully reinstating Absalom in David's favor after
the murder of Amnon (2 Samuel 14:1-20). But on several occasions, he
did things against the will of David like killing Abner, who was trying
to bring the rest of the country under David's authority. But, because
of a personal revenge, Joab killed him and at the same occasion putting
David's kingship in danger (2 Samuel 3:26-30). Joab killed David's
nephew, and own cousin Amasa, after David appointed him as the new
chief of staff (2 Samuel 20:8-12). He killed Absalom when he revolted,
but it was against David's command to not touch him. David
understood that you do not kill your own sons no matter what they do,
but Joab could not grasp how important that was for David (2 Samuel
18:9-15) And, finally, Joab did not follow David's choice for
succession, because David had chosen Solomon, but Joab went on
Adonijah's side (1 Kings 2:28). Friends can kill your sons when you
don't pay attention like he killed Absalom.

FRIENDS THINK ABOUT YOUR PRESENT
AND NOT REALLY YOUR FUTURE

The paradox of vision is, even if a vision is not given to a group, it is given to an individual. No true vision can be fulfilled by just the visionary, but by a group of people. And, this is where servants, friends, and sons come in. What the Bible tells us concerning what to do once you receive a vision in Habakkuk 2:2, is to write it down in such a way that those who run with the vision can do it easily. Notice that the ones who write the vision down are not the ones who run with it. To write the vision down implies to sit down, assess what is needed for the vision, and plan for it. This task is for a father and his friends. This is where many people get confused. Because many times those who receive the vision, try to run with it. That is why Moses tried to cross the Jordan and take the people himself in to the Promised Land. Naturally, fathers are more patient and have a lot more experience than sons, so sitting down and planning is really fit for them. A father will mainly need his friends to help him come up with a good plan for his vision. On the other hand, sons are naturally fit to run and make things happen. They have more energy and a spirit of getting things done. They don't need all the answers before they can move.

The problem is that when the father's generation (the father and his friends) does not do their job of planning and putting the vision down on tablets and they try to run instead, nature itself makes sure they do not have that much energy and there will not be much result and no plan at the same time because the time they should have been planning, but they were trying to run. Now, when it is time for the sons to run, there is nothing planned and written down, so the sons are going to waste their energy trying to come up with a plan; and at the same time they are not so well equipped for that, which will frustrate them. And at the end of the day, God has lost two generations because no one was doing what he was supposed to be doing.

The other danger is when you leave your friends with your sons without defining a proper role of each one in your legacy. Remember, friends are only faithful to you and not necessarily to what belongs to you – your vision. They helped you to plan not necessarily because of the dedication to the vision, but to you. And, being faithful to the vision rather than the visionary can make a huge difference. For example, Moses was so faithful to God's vision that he opposed Him when he wanted to destroy the people because they were not obeying. Of course, God was just testing Moses to see where his heart was, but the point is that a son can oppose a father for the benefit of the father's vision. To protect your legacy, you need to make sure to separate what you leave for your friends when you hand the baton to your sons. Friends can counsel and support your sons but they cannot work together as they did with you. Friends will never submit to your sons, and sons will not submit to your friends either. Sons will obey and follow your instructions without questioning, but friends will have their own opinion.

Now the opinion of your friends is very good for you while you are still there to judge if that is fit for your vision and sometimes it can be very beneficial, especially if you are not right because friends can correct you and not sons, but it will be a huge problem if the friends are not dealing with you but they are dealing with your sons. Because David had understood this principle when he was dealing with Joab, who was dedicated to David, he rightfully corrected him when Absalom died, as we can read in the book of 2 Samuel 19,

"It was told Joab, 'Behold, the king is weeping and mourning for Absalom.' So, the victory that day was turned into mourning for all the people, for the people heard that day, 'The king is grieving for his son.' And the people stole into the city that day as people steal in who are ashamed when they flee in battle. The king covered his face, and the king cried with a loud voice, 'O my son Absalom, O Absalom, my son, my son!' Then Joab came into the house to the king and said, 'You have today covered with shame the faces of all your servants, who have this day saved your life and the lives of your sons and your daughters

and the lives of your wives and your concubines, because you love those who hate you and hate those who love you. For you have made it clear today that commanders and servants are nothing to you, for today I know that if Absalom were alive and all of us were dead today, then you would be pleased. Now therefore arise, go out and speak kindly to your servants, for I swear by the Lord, if you do not go, not a man will stay with you this night, and this will be worse for you than all the evil that has come upon you from your youth until now.' Then the king arose and took his seat in the gate. And the people were all told, 'Behold, the king is sitting in the gate.' And all the people came before the king."

But as he was not concerned by David's future, when David was leaving Solomon in charge he asked him to make sure Joab is out of the picture (1 Kings 2:5-6). Time to time, friends question what you say. That is why they can hardly ever learn from you. In the times of Jesus, the Pharisees considered themselves to be his equals. They were all rabbis, so they never submitted to him. I will not say that they were his friends because they did not even get too close to know what was on his heart, but my point is that their hearts and positions made it impossible for them to learn anything from Jesus. What some people know can prevent them from becoming sons. Sons must have the heart and mind like a child. Children may lack knowledge but they are eager and hungry to learn all that they can. They naturally hunger to learn. They want to learn from you all that you know. This is why Jesus went to those who did not have much spiritual knowledge. He chose fishermen.

If you build your legacy with friends, you will have people who do not know a lot about your vision because they were too familiar to learn from you. And because of this, they will fight with your sons. There is nothing that can destroy a vision faster than more than one vision in any place. That is called division. Sons know far more about your vision than friends because they were like empty computer drives with a very high download speed. Sons have a very high absorption rate because of their disposition to learn from you, and you have friends or even brothers on the other hand who have more authority because, remember, they are in a higher position than your sons, but they do not know much because they can hardly learn from you. They are too familiar and assume they know what you know or even know better than you. Leaving your legacy without making sure your friends and brothers are not going to hinder your sons to materialize your dream will limit or even cancel the impact of your vision. The best and only thing to do is to make your friends the counselors and advisors of your sons. You put them in a position where they can give their input when your sons need some of their knowledge because your sons still need those who have experience and have been with you when you were putting down the vision. Most of the time, your friends know more about your past than your sons, which makes them a very good resource, but they are not really built for your future. They are not built to run your vision. Only sons inherit from their fathers anyway.

ONLY SONS ARE THERE FOR YOUR FUTURE

Isn't it interesting how Jesus did not leave the church in the hands of the disciple he loved, the one we can say was his friend? The apostle John is said to have been the one he loved and who was reclining on Jesus' bosom. But, Jesus left him in charge of his mother and not the vision. Your friends and brothers take care of your family and not your vision. They protect your past and not your future. Only sons protect your future. Friends should make sure your sons run the vision smoothly and support them but are not running it with them. It is very easy to be tempted to want your friends even yourself to run with your sons because you may see your sons as still too young and too inexperienced to handle what is laid down for them, but trust your DNA in them, trust that they have what it takes to take the vision on the next level. Remember that it is better to leave too soon than to stay too long. You know it is time to leave the scene and hand the baton to your sons when you know that the resources you have are not enough to respond to the present demand the vision is putting on you.

Like we saw Moses felt that the demand was too high for him to handle, but because he did not understand that is the sign to prepare the next generation and let them run, he thought it was his time to die. The same thing happened to Elijah. Do not die without preparing and handing the baton to the next generation. Jesus came on the earth to save the whole world by re-introducing the Kingdom of God. He understood well that is what his dream was, and he personally focused on the Jews. When the gentiles started to put demand on him, He knew it was time to leave the rest of the mission to his sons – the apostles. John 12:20-24,

> *"Now there were some Greeks among the people who had come up to give worship at the feast: They came to Philip, who was of Bethsaida in Galilee, and made a request, saying, 'Sir, we have a desire to see Jesus.' Philip went and gave word of it to Andrew; and Andrew went with Philip to Jesus. And Jesus said to them in answer, 'The hour of the glory of the Son of man has come. Truly I say to you, if a seed of grain does not go into the earth and come to an end, it is still a seed and no more; but through its death it gives much fruit.'"*

When Jesus heard that the Greeks were now interested in seeing him He understood it was time to pass on the baton. Unfortunately, many fathers die with the baton in their hands to the point that the sons must fight to get it from their dead cold hands. David was the greatest King of Israel not only because of his achievements, but because he is the only King that left the throne because it was time to handoff the baton and not because he was dead. He had enough time to prepare his son Solomon to succeed him and even prepared his friends to be who they were supposed to be for Solomon. David had time to give instructions to his son on how he should deal with his friends. He warned Solomon that he should make sure he did not let Joab stay around. He knew he was not going to able to handle him as a son. 1 Kings 2:3-10 states,

> *"Do the job the Lord your God has assigned you by following his instructions and obeying his rules, commandments, regulations, and laws as written in the law of Moses. Then you will succeed in all you do and*

seek to accomplish, and the Lord will fulfill his promise to me, if your descendants watch their step and live faithfully in my presence with all their heart and being, then, he promised, you will not fail to have a successor on the throne of Israel. You know what Joab son of Zeruiah did to me - how he murdered two commanders of the Israelite armies, Abner son of Ner and Amasa son of Jether. During peacetime, he struck them down like he would in battle; when he shed their blood as if in battle, he stained his own belt and the sandals on his feet. Do to him what you think is appropriate, but don't let him live long and die a peaceful death. Treat fairly the sons of Barzillai of Gilead and provide for their needs, because they helped me when I had to flee from your brother Absalom. Note well, you still have to contend with Shimei son of Gera, the Benjamite from Bahurim, who tried to call down upon me a horrible judgment when I went to Mahanaim. He came down and met me at the Jordan, and I solemnly promised him by the Lord, I will not strike you down with the sword. But now don't treat him as if he were innocent. You are a wise man and you know how to handle him; make sure he has a bloody death.' Then David passed away and was buried in the city of David."

REVIEW OF PRINCIPLES OF SONSHIP

Principles of Sonship are so important that you cannot fulfill God's command to have dominion over the earth without a proper understanding and application of all of them. According to Genesis 1:28, "God blessed them: and God said unto them, 'Be fruitful, and multiply, and replenish the earth, and subdue it; and have dominion over the fish of the sea, and over the birds of the heavens, and over every living thing that moves upon the earth.'" Having dominion over the earth comes in stages, the first one being to be fruitful, or to make the seed God created you with grow. Now, this step cannot be reached without proper submission to someone else. Luke 16:12 reminds us that if you have not been faithful to what belongs to someone else, nobody can give you what belongs to you. This is when you abandon for a time your vision, or I should say, you bury your seed into the ground while you are serving your fathers vision. Without understanding and applying this principle of sonship, you cannot be fruitful. Now, this does not mean that you cannot do anything. It simply means that you cannot live or produce up to your full potential. If you are not applying these principles of sonship, whatever you are doing is not what you could or should have done if you applied them. That is why you may be feeling frustrated because deep inside you know you have more to offer; you feel that you could have done better. After you have become fruitful, comes the stage of multiplication of your fruits. This stage is accomplished by duplicating yourself or producing sons who will carry your vision. The more sons you have, the bigger your impact is. Only then can you cover the whole domain where you are supposed to influence, subdue it, and have dominion over it through your sons. Remember that our God thinks in generations. Whatever starts with you is to be finished in generations to come, and without sonship there are no generations. Many times in the Bible, the blessing or favor of God is attached to having children. This is because God is always thinking about legacy. And, do you remember when God told Abraham that He would bless him? Abraham's reaction was, "How are you going to bless me if I can't have sons?" He understood that you need sons and not servants for you to be really blessed, and God agreed with him. When God was mad at someone, He would make them barren because He is a God of generations. No matter what you do, you cannot fulfill all God has for you during your lifetime, and the only way to continue and finish what He has for you is to have sons who will build your legacy.

As we saw it, one of the promises God gave to the children of Israel was that if they obeyed his laws, no barren woman or man would be found in their midst. Jesus mastered sonship. As a matter of fact, he said that He has given us God's name and that is "Our Father" so we can be his sons. But, before he could reintroduce the "Heavenly Father" to us, He became a "Son" Himself – first to his parents at the age of 12 when he made a decision to follow them back home from the temple and submit and serve them for 18 years and secondly to John the Baptist when he submitted to his vision and assignment and then produced sons that carried his dream to save the world by reintroducing the "Kingdom" back to mankind!

The difference between Jesus (the last Adam) and the first Adam was sonship. Adam was created grown up. He did not have anyone to submit to so that he could develop his character. No wonder why at the first test he could not submit to God because he had not been trained and developed. I can imagine God the Father saying before He sends Jesus to the earth, "This time I just must make sure He is born in a family and go through all the stages of sonship, then He will be able to submit to me and accomplish my assignment!" Sonship is the master key to unlock your destiny! Master it, and (as my father, Dr. Munroe, would say) I will see you at the top!

Hubert Sugira Hategekimana
Author / Business Consultant / Inspirational Speaker

Ask Hubert about the importance of discovering your leadership potential and you will get a mile wide smile and a rousing discussion about how fulfillment and success are found when you develop a vision for your life according to your purpose.

As a native of Rwanda and survivor of the 1994 genocide, which took the lives of over one million people in 100 days, Hubert Sugira Hategekimana knows firsthand how oppressive leadership philosophies can cause calamity and atrocity to individuals, communities, and nations. With strong convictions and a hopeful heart, he teaches leadership principles that empower rather than oppress, focus on character instead of charisma, and encourage a biblical based perspective of self.

Hubert is a cross-cultural leader, whose life journey has taken him from Rwanda to Europe and Canada. He has a passion for connecting people to their destiny by focusing on the process of self-fulfillment – from purpose discovery to vision attainment.

Hubert has undergone extensive training in the areas of self-discovery and leadership development under the tutelage of world-renowned government consultant and best-selling author, the late Dr. Myles Munroe. He had the privilege of traveling with Dr. Munroe, accompanying him to private sessions with diplomats and government officials in Kenya, Uganda, and Burundi.

Hubert has been a featured speaker at multiple leadership conferences across the globe including Europe, Africa, North America, and the Caribbean. His signature teaching, *Power & Principles of Sonship*, helps individuals identify and unlock their area of leadership gifting through proper submission and honor to authority.

Living and applying these principles has also caused Hubert to excel in business. After beginning as an entry level Sales Representative, he broke the company record and became an Executive Business Developer in one short year.

Hubert is a Trustee of the International Third World Leaders Association (ITWLA), a global network of leaders changing the destiny of nations through leadership training and development, which was founded by the late Dr. Myles Munroe. He also serves as the Assistant Pastor and mentor at his local church, under the direction of Pastor Arsene Poungui, where he teaches Kingdom principles for impactful living.

Like any perpetual student, Hubert loves connecting with like-minded leaders to discuss ideas of change and transformation for the world. He attributes his success to the love, support, and wisdom of his best friend and wife, Jennifer. Hubert and his wife reside in Ottawa, Ontario (Canada) with their three beautiful children, Kayla, Ketsia, and Klemes.

Website: Hategekimana.com
Email: Hubert@Hategekimana.com
www.facebook.com/HubertSugira
YouTube: Hubert Sugira Hategekimana
Twitter: @SugiraHubert
#Sonship #TheKingsWay
#TheKingdomLifeStyle
#TrainedByTheBest

Made in the USA
Middletown, DE
24 September 2021